BOOK D

My Spelling Workbook

This book belongs to:

....

My Spelling Workbook *(Book D)*

Published by Prim-Ed Publishing 2011
3rd edition 2021
Reprinted 2015, 2021, 2022, 2023, 2024, 2025, 2026
Copyright© Prim-Ed Publishing 2011
ISBN 978-1-80087-111-3
PR–2283

Titles available in this series:
My Spelling Workbook *(Book A)*
My Spelling Workbook *(Book B)*
My Spelling Workbook *(Book C)*
My Spelling Workbook *(Book D)*
My Spelling Workbook *(Book E)*
My Spelling Workbook *(Book F)*
My Spelling Workbook *(Book G)*

Offices in:

UK and Republic of Ireland:
Unit 2A, Block E
Waterford Road Business Park
New Ross, Co. Wexford
Y34 NC82, Ireland
www.prim-ed.com

Australia:
PO Box 332, Greenwood
Western Australia 6924
www.ricpublications.com.au

Disclaimer

Every effort has been made to ensure quality of content and accuracy of information; our team at R.I.C. Publications® and Prim-Ed Publishing cannot be held responsible for mistakes or omissions, but we do endeavour to rectify any errors found within our products. Please contact us to provide feedback.

Introduction

Welcome to *My Spelling Workbook*.

This book and interactive download have lots of activities to help you learn to spell.

You should follow this method when you are learning to spell each word.

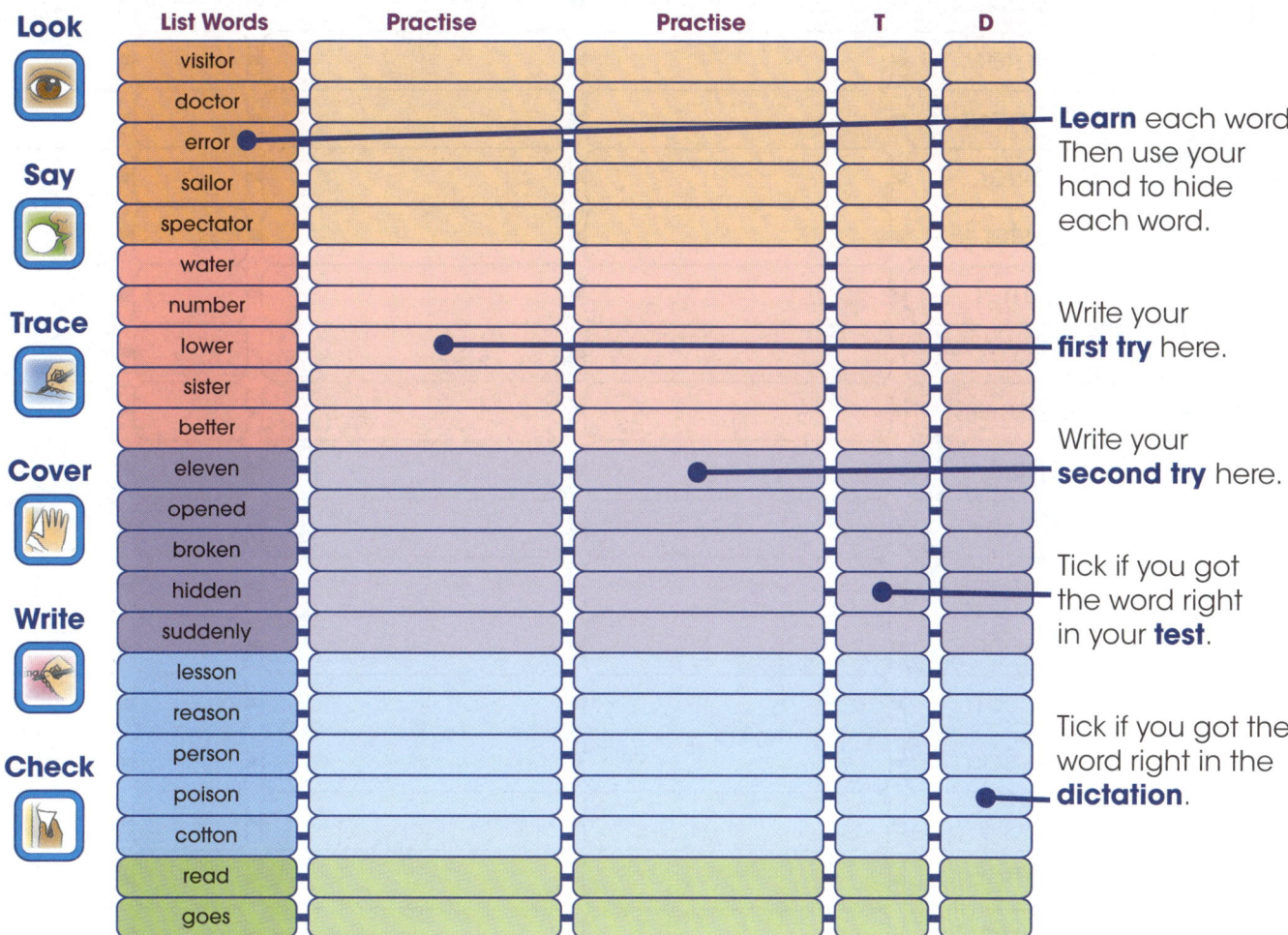

Look

Say

Trace

Cover

Write

Check

Learn each word. Then use your hand to hide each word.

Write your **first try** here.

Write your **second try** here.

Tick if you got the word right in your **test**.

Tick if you got the word right in the **dictation**.

List Words: visitor, doctor, error, sailor, spectator, water, number, lower, sister, better, eleven, opened, broken, hidden, suddenly, lesson, reason, person, poison, cotton, read, goes

Contents

Unit 1

or er en on

List Words	Practise	Practise	T	D
visitor				
doctor				
error				
sailor				
spectator				
water				
number				
lower				
sister				
better				
eleven				
opened				
broken				
hidden				
suddenly				
lesson				
reason				
person				
poison				
cotton				
read				
goes				

Antonyms

1. Find a list word with an opposite meaning.

   (a) comes _____

   (b) closed _____

   (c) higher _____

   (d) worse _____

   (e) gradually _____

   (f) brother _____

Missing Letters

2. Use 'or', 'er', 'en' or 'on' to complete the list words.

   (a) elev___ ___

   (b) less___ ___

   (c) pois___ ___

   (d) bett___ ___

   (e) err___ ___

   (f) reas___ ___

My Spelling Workbook D—Prim-Ed Publishing—www.prim-ed.com

CROSSWORD

3. Use list words to solve the crossword.

Across

5. Good, _____, best.

7. A mistake.

8. Smashed or destroyed.

12. A material or thread.

13. A human being.

14. A caller or guest.

17. I have a tennis _____ every Saturday.

19. To understand something written.

20. Quickly.

21. A person who watches a show or game.

Down

1. 9, 6 or 5.

2. Out of sight or unseen.

3. Colourless liquid.

4. 20 minus 9.

6. Low, _____, lowest.

9. Visits if you are ill.

10. I go, we go and he _____.

11. Opposite of closed.

13. A dangerous substance.

15. A person who sails.

16. She had no _____ to be angry with him.

18. Boy is to brother as girl is to _____.

Base Words

A **base word** is a word in its simplest form. A base word has nothing added to it; e.g. do, heat, write, read, pack.

> Look at this word: **visitor**
> The base word for this is **visit**.

4. Find the base word for the following words. Remember some of these words are irregular.

(a) sailor _____

(b) spectator _____

(c) goes _____

(d) lower _____

(e) hidden _____

(f) broken _____

(g) opened _____

(h) better _____

Unit 1

List Words

visitor
doctor
error
sailor
spectator
water
number
lower
sister
better
eleven
opened
broken
hidden
suddenly
lesson
reason
person
poison
cotton
read
goes

Missing Words

5. Complete the sentences using the list or revision words.

(a) My older _____ is _____

at spelling than I am.

(b) You _____ go to the _____

when you are ill.

(c) The _____ watched the tragic

_____ made by the racing driver.

(d) He had to _____ long and

hard at his ski _____.

Secret Words

6. Find the secret words.

(a) Put '**t**' in front of '**error**'. _____

(b) Take '**ch**' off '**chew**' and put in '**cr**'. _____

(c) Take '**c**' off '**clue**' and put in '**g**'. _____

(d) Take '**tor**' off '**spectator**' and
put in '**cles**'. _____

(e) Take '**s**' off '**sister**' and put in '**bl**'. _____

Word Track

7. Cross out every second letter to make
two list or revision words.

Revision Words

chew
few
due
clue
spoon
bathroom
comic
picnic
should
work

WORD SEARCH

8. Find the list and revision words in the word search.

visitor	doctor
error	sailor
spectator	water
number	lower
sister	better
eleven	opened
broken	hidden
suddenly	lesson
reason	person
poison	cotton
read	goes
chew	few
due	clue
spoon	bathroom
comic	picnic
should	work

```
p i c n i c n x l e s s o n t
u w b e t t e r u c o t t o n
j o s h o u l d p u v r f f r
b r o k e n e a n e d d i h o
w k v m x l n o s i o p g i l
s u d d e n l y c i m o c r i
t j a v t s p e c t a t o r a
j p e m o o r h t a b t w w s
n n o s a e r n s n i w n y d
e u l c n y e a j s v i z n r
e t m s k o w s i s t e r o z
c r f b e x o v d a e r t s d
h l r h e o l p s e h c y r h
e t t o y r g z s c o g f e w
w a t e r m q i s d e n e p o
```

WORD HUNT

9. Which list or revision word(s) …

(a) is an anagram of '**dear**'?

_____

(b) have the sound '**oo**'?

_____

_____

(c) is an uneven number?

_____

(d) have three letters?

_____

_____

Changing Words

10. Change one letter in each word to make a list or revision word.

(a) wore   _____

(b) tower   _____

(c) glue   _____

(d) season   _____

(e) crew   _____

(f) wafer   _____

Additional Activities

11. (a) Write all the nouns.

(b) Change the nouns to verbs where possible.

(c) Write sentences, each containing one of these verbs.

Unit 2

List Words	Practise	Practise	T	D
hoof				
leaf				
beef				
scarf				
elf				
golf				
wolf				
shelf				
half				
calf				
safe				
wife				
life				
oxen				
geese				
dice				
children				
women				
teeth				
feet				
large				
does				

Singular Words

1. These words are irregular plurals.
    Write the singular of these words.

    (a) feet _____

    (b) geese _____

    (c) teeth _____

    (d) children _____

    (e) oxen _____

    (f) women _____

    (g) dice _____

All Mixed Up

2. Unjumble the list words.

    (a) faes _____

    (b) galer _____

    (c) efeb _____

    (d) sode _____

    (e) cied _____

    (f) olgf _____

    (g) hlefs _____

CROSSWORD

3. Use list words to solve the crossword.

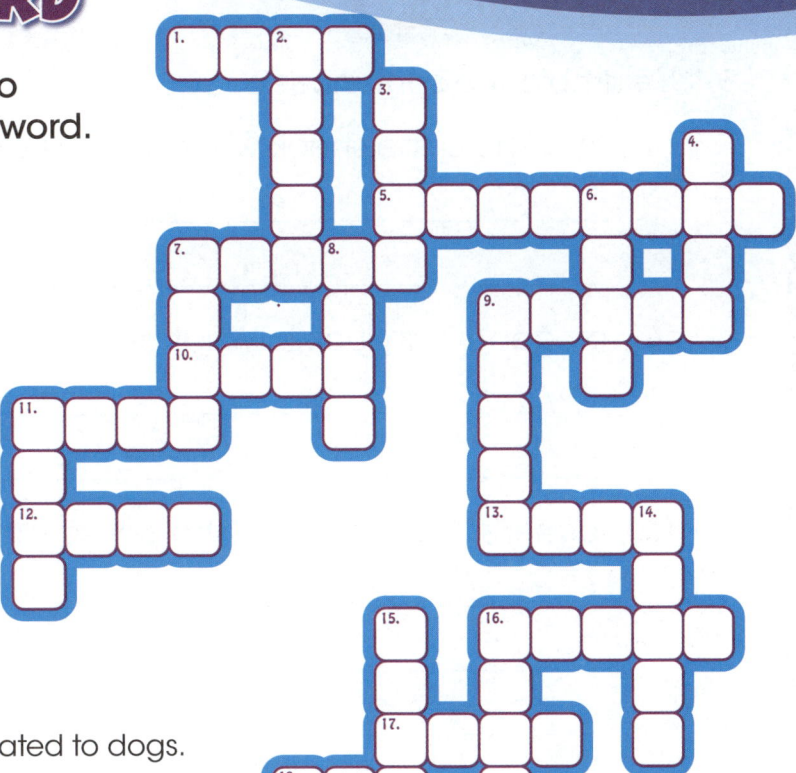

Across

1. Wild animal related to dogs.
5. Plural of child.
7. Birds with long necks and short legs.
9. A ledge for holding things.
10. Flat, green part of a plant or tree.
11. One of two equal parts.
12. Plural of ox.
13. They have ten toes.
16. Females.
17. Is there _____ on Mars?
18. Small mischievous fairy.

Down

2. Big.
3. Plural of a small cube with numbers 1 to 6.
4. Flesh of a cow used for food.
6. I do, we do and he _____.
7. A sport using a club and small ball.
8. Free from danger or risk.
9. It keeps your neck warm.
11. A horse's foot.
14. Plural of tooth.
15. A young cow.
16. Man is to husband as woman is to _____.

More Than One

Rule: Words ending in 'f' or 'fe' change the 'f' to 'v' and add 'es'.

Exceptions: Some words ending in 'f' cannot make their minds up. Sometimes they change 'f' to 'v' and add 'es'; at other times they just add 's'.

4. Make these words plural.

(a) wife _____

(b) scarf _____

(c) half _____

(d) hoof _____

(e) shelf _____

(f) wolf _____

Unit 2

List Words

hoof
leaf
beef
scarf
elf
golf
wolf
shelf
half
calf
safe
wife
life
oxen
geese
dice
children
women
teeth
feet
large
does

Revision Words

love
oven
other
Monday
onion
front
luck
shock
Ireland
March

Mixed-up Sentences

5. Unjumble the sentences.

(a) they The a the shock when wolf. saw children had

_____

_____

(b) on good 17th luck to What be Ireland Monday March. in

_____

_____

(c) farmer's The to sell. wife the geese market to took

_____

_____

_____

Shape Sorter

6. Write the word that fits in each shape.

(a)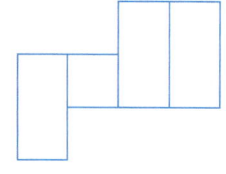

(b)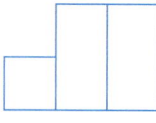

(c)

(d)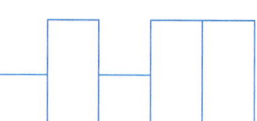

Antonyms

7. Find a list or revision word with the opposite meaning.

(a) back _____

(b) husband _____

(c) hate _____

(d) dangerous _____

(e) death _____

(f) adults _____

WORD SEARCH

8. Find the list and revision words in the word search.

hoof
beef
elf
wolf
half
safe
life
geese
children
feet
does
oven
Monday
front
shock
women

leaf
scarf
golf
shelf
calf
wife
oxen
dice
teeth
large
love
other
onion
luck
March
Ireland

r	x	f	l	o	g	c	s	s	t	r	v	n	d	s	g	M
w	o	m	e	n	i	q	r	h	u	d	o	r	i	z	o	n
n	r	r	l	e	v	o	l	a	t	d	n	d	e	n	b	c
r	e	o	h	x	g	x	l	l	t	n	w	a	d	e	n	i
p	e	r	s	x	e	e	i	f	e	h	o	a	l	o	l	g
h	d	h	d	h	u	n	f	y	e	x	y	r	i	e	j	u
c	w	f	t	l	o	l	e	c	t	e	q	n	f	q	r	s
b	r	M	s	o	i	c	l	a	h	m	o	d	e	t	x	l
d	h	u	a	h	c	h	k	l	g	g	w	t	e	e	f	u
h	y	l	o	r	e	o	c	f	d	p	g	e	b	l	f	s
i	v	g	t	g	c	l	i	y	i	m	v	s	q	l	a	e
f	x	c	r	n	f	h	f	s	c	m	x	e	e	f	o	k
b	r	a	w	e	b	z	u	w	e	s	w	e	e	f	k	j
e	l	a	s	v	s	e	o	d	d	m	p	g	x	l	j	k
h	x	k	c	o	m	u	s	u	f	o	o	h	p	o	j	t
x	a	v	l	s	e	a	i	c	w	g	e	f	i	w	b	f
e	m	q	r	j	q	k	i	e	l	e	a	f	l	u	c	k

Magic Words

9. Change the first word into the last by changing one letter on each line to make a new word.

For example: rate
                race
                rice
                dice

(a)   loft

        _____

        _____

        life

(b)   hill

        _____

        _____

        half

Changing Words

10. Change one letter in the words below to make a list or revision word.

(a) omen   _____

(b) wine   _____

(c) calm   _____

(d) scare   _____

(e) line   _____

Additional Activities

11. (a) Write the revision list words in alphabetical order. Check your spelling.

(b) Choose five list words and write a sentence containing each word.

(c) Choose five different list words. Use a dictionary to write a definition for each word.

Unit 3

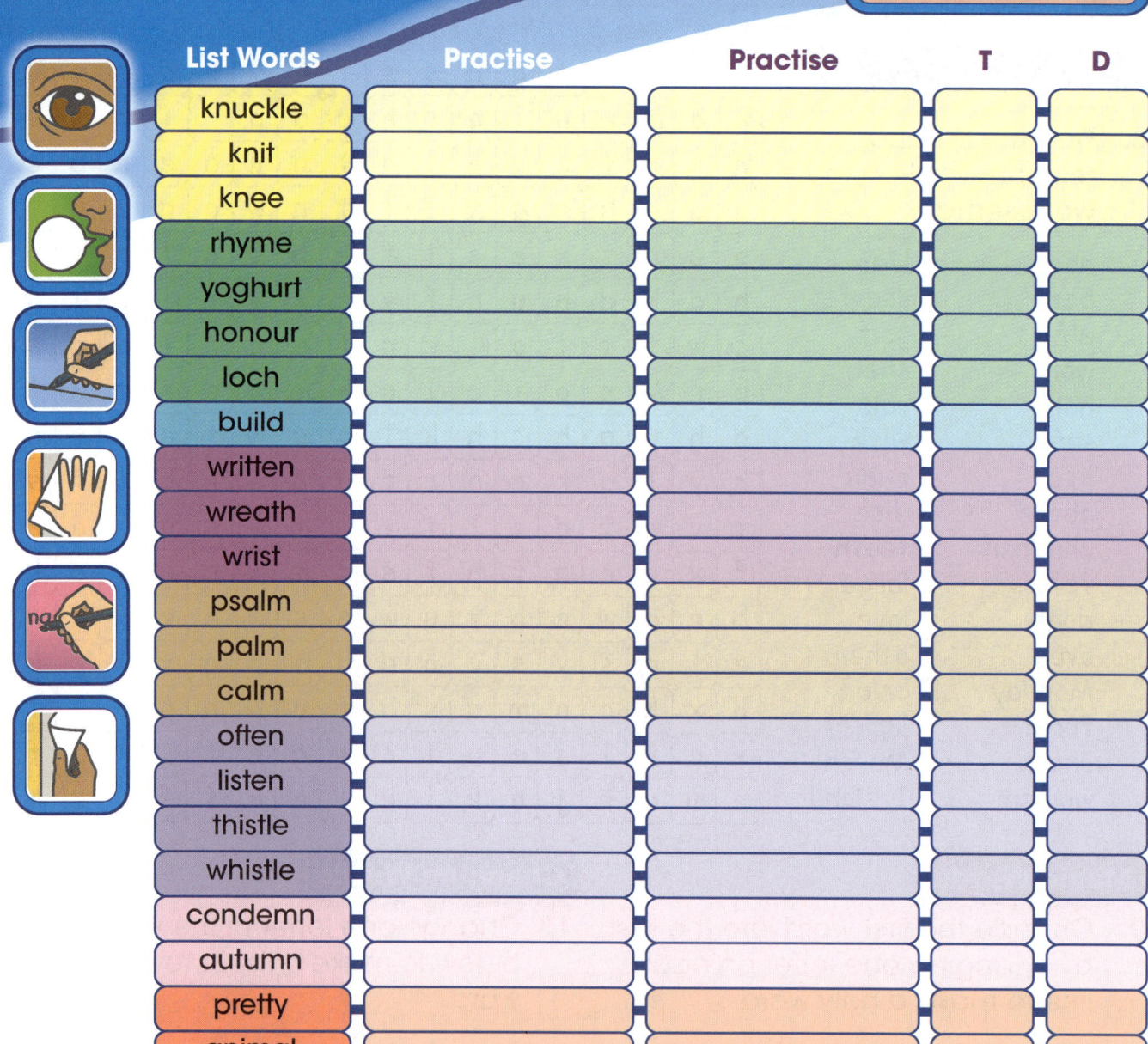

List Words	Practise	Practise	T	D
knuckle				
knit				
knee				
rhyme				
yoghurt				
honour				
loch				
build				
written				
wreath				
wrist				
psalm				
palm				
calm				
often				
listen				
thistle				
whistle				
condemn				
autumn				
pretty				
animal				

Silent Letters

1. Write the list words next to the correct headings.

(a) Silent 't'

(b) Silent 'k'

(c) Silent 'l'

(d) Silent 'n'

(e) Silent 'h'

(f) Silent 'u'

(g) Silent 'w'

Silent Letters

CROSSWORD

2. Use list words to solve the crossword.

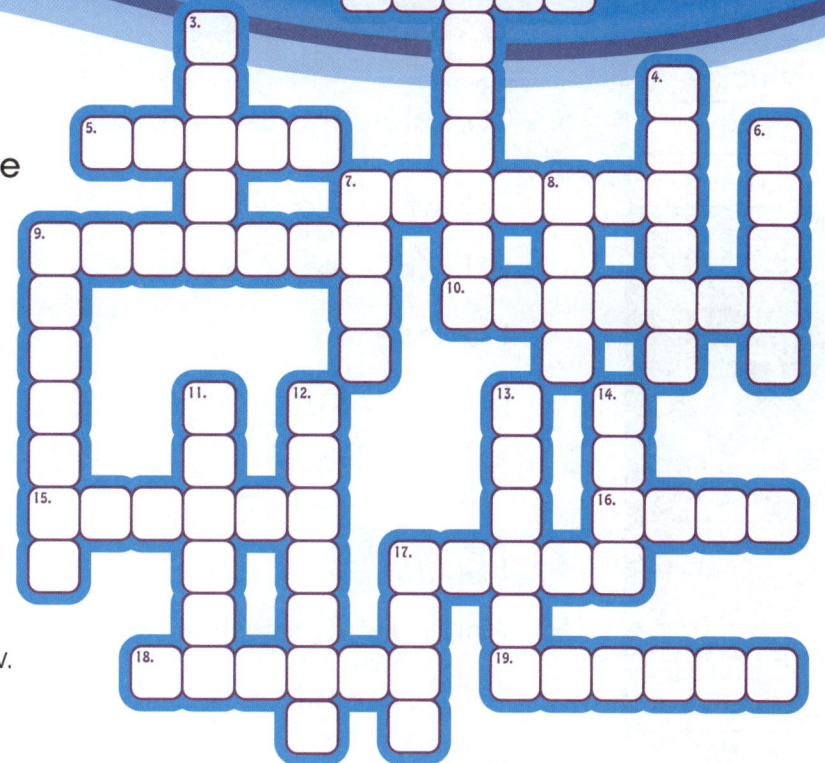

Across

1. cat, sat, fat, rat, bat, mat.
5. Putting things together.
7. Part of the finger.
9. The past participle of 'write'.
10. National flower of Scotland.
15. Hear.
16. A Scottish lake.
17. A hymn.
18. A lion, a dog, a horse or a cow.
19. High respect.

Down

2. A sour, thick liquid made from milk.
3. The joint connecting a hand to an arm.
4. Attractive, lovely.
6. Frequently.
7. A joint on the leg.
8. Using needles to make wool into items of clothing.
9. A high-pitched sound.
11. The season after summer.
12. To disapprove or criticize.
13. A ring made of flowers and leaves.
14. Peaceful, mild, restful.
17. The flat surface of the hand.

Adding Endings

3. Finish the table by adding the suffixes 's' and 'ing' and writing the past tense. The words with an asterisk * have a special rule to remember.

Verb	Add 's'	Add 'ing'	Past tense
listen	listens		
*build			built
*knot			
*rhyme		rhyming	
*write			wrote *or* have _____

Rule 1: With '**rhyme**' and '**write**', ___ goes away when ___ comes to stay.

Rule 2: With '**knot**', the letter ___ is doubled when adding '**ing**' and '**ed**', to keep the vowel sound short.

Rule 3: The word '**build**' becomes _____ in the past tense.

Unit 3

List Words

knuckle
knit
knee
rhyme
yoghurt
honour
loch
build
written
wreath
wrist
psalm
palm
calm
often
listen
thistle
whistle
condemn
autumn
pretty
animal

Revision Words

alive
thank
supply
apply
cried
tried
high
right
while
which

Missing Letters

4. Complete the list or revision words.

(a) whis___le

(b) wh___le

(c) pa___m

(d) p___alm

(e) w___ich

(f) condem___

(g) loc___

(h) ___reath

(i) a___ply

Synonyms

5. Find a list or revision word with a similar meaning.

(a) frequently _____

(b) creature _____

(c) provide _____

(d) correct _____

Word Whistle

6. Cross out every second letter.
The leftover letters will make three list or revision words.

_____ _____

pfrhegthtayccloanbdhekmrnptsrrimegd

Proofreading

7. Circle the incorrect words and rewrite them correctly in the spaces.

(a) I tryed to lisen for the wistle wile playing the game.

_____ _____

_____ _____

(b) He cryed when the baby on his nee bit his nuckle.

_____ _____ _____

WORD SEARCH

8. Find the list and revision words in the word search.

knuckle	knit	knee
rhyme	yoghurt	honour
loch	build	written
wreath	wrist	psalm
palm	calm	often
listen	thistle	whistle
condemn	autumn	pretty
animal	alive	thank
supply	apply	cried
tried	high	right
	while	which

w	h	i	c	h	n	d	n	h	q	s	x	y	u	t
y	e	f	k	e	k	y	e	n	f	k	p	t	s	j
a	y	g	t	n	o	j	f	i	b	n	y	t	b	j
p	d	s	a	n	i	m	a	l	r	u	l	e	d	f
p	i	o	s	x	j	t	m	l	a	c	p	r	d	n
l	w	r	i	s	t	t	h	a	n	k	p	p	e	m
y	h	s	t	r	h	y	m	e	n	l	u	a	i	e
p	i	q	h	i	n	p	t	e	r	e	s	n	r	d
k	l	e	i	l	z	f	e	i	e	r	b	y	t	n
a	e	l	s	d	o	m	g	w	u	v	o	l	e	o
u	u	t	t	a	l	h	l	o	r	g	i	t	m	c
t	l	s	l	s	t	i	n	a	h	e	t	l	i	h
u	o	i	e	g	u	o	u	u	s	i	a	k	a	p
m	c	h	g	i	h	l	r	b	r	p	d	t	o	m
n	h	w	n	d	z	t	p	w	o	y	p	x	h	b

Missing Words

9. Complete the sentences using the list or revision words.

(a) My grandma is going to _____ me a _____ jumper.

(b) The council are planning to _____ a café next to the

_____.

(c) The _____ will hibernate at the end of _____.

(d) The priest had _____ a new _____ to read in church.

(e) We had to _____ to my sister's baby when it _____ all last night.

Rhyming Words

10. Write list or revision words that rhyme with these words.

(a) kitten _____

(b) stitch _____

(c) tree _____

(d) time _____

(e) sigh _____

(f) filled _____

(g) night _____

(h) cannibal _____

Additional Activities

11. (a) Find ten more words with silent letters. Check your spelling.

(b) Write the meanings of your new words.

(c) Write each of your new words in a sentence.

Unit 4

List Words	Practise	Practise	T	D
fair				
stair				
chair				
hairy				
airy				
dairy				
pair				
repair				
despair				
pushchair				
dare				
scare				
beware				
glare				
fare				
stare				
care				
rare				
spare				
mare				
Belfast				
Dublin				

Compound Words

1. Add the correct list word to make compound words.

   (a) arm_____

   (b) _____case

   (c) _____devil

   (d) night_____

   (e) _____crow

   (f) air_____

   (g) _____free

Missing Letters

2. Use 'air' or 'are' to complete the list words.

   (a) h___ ___ ___y

   (b) gl___ ___ ___

   (c) rep___ ___ ___

   (d) bew___ ___ ___

   (e) desp___ ___ ___

   (f) d___ ___ ___y

   (g) p___ ___ ___

My Spelling Workbook D—Prim-Ed Publishing—www.prim-ed.com

CROSSWORD

3. Use list words to solve the crossword.

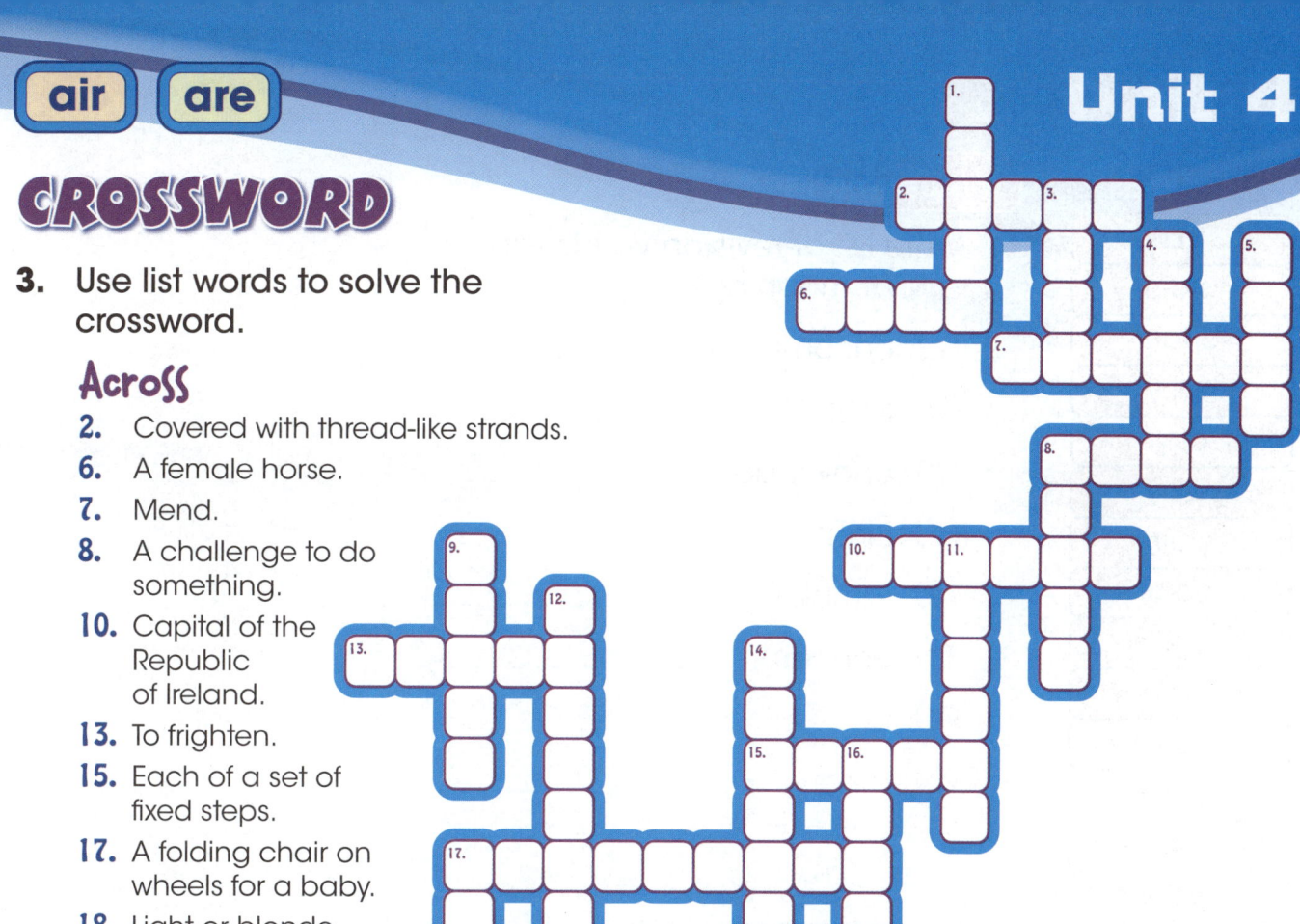

Across

2. Covered with thread-like strands.

6. A female horse.

7. Mend.

8. A challenge to do something.

10. Capital of the Republic of Ireland.

13. To frighten.

15. Each of a set of fixed steps.

17. A folding chair on wheels for a baby.

18. Light or blonde.

19. The money a passenger pays.

Down

1. Extra to what is needed.

3. Not happening very often.

4. A seat.

5. To look after someone.

8. _____ products are made from milk.

9. To stare in an angry way.

11. Look out!

12. Capital city of Northern Ireland.

14. A total loss of hope.

16. Full of fresh air and light.

17. Two.

Homophones

Homophones are words that sound the same but have a different spelling and a different meaning; e.g. to, two and too. 'I go to school'; 'We have two cars'; 'Sam was too hot'.

4. Write the correct homophone from the list words to complete the sentences.

(a) It is bad manners to _____ at someone.

(b) When I stepped on the _____ it made a loud creak.

(c) My dad gives me money for my bus _____ every day.

(d) We had great fun on the roller coaster at the _____.

Unit 4

List Words

fair
stair
chair
hairy
airy
dairy
pair
repair
despair
pushchair
dare
scare
beware
glare
fare
stare
care
rare
spare
mare
Belfast
Dublin

Revision Words

smell
stall
glass
across
buzz
dizzy
staff
stuff
yesterday
April

Synonyms

5. Write list or revision words with similar meanings.

(a) uncommon _____

(b) faint _____

(c) challenge _____

(d) fright _____

(e) tumbler _____

(f) concern _____

(g) fix _____

(h) misery _____

More Than One

Rule: To make the plural of words ending with a 'y' after a consonant, change the 'y' to 'i' and add 'es'.

6. Make the following words plural.

(a) glass _____ (b) mare _____

(c) smell _____ (d) dairy _____

(e) pushchair _____ (f) stair _____

(g) repair _____ (h) pair _____

WORD HUNT

7. Which list or revision word(s) ...

(a) are capital cities? _____

(b) has a sound that suggests the meaning of the word? _____

(c) is a compound word? _____

(d) refer to 'time'? _____

(e) start with 'a'? _____

WORD SEARCH

8. Find the list and revision words in the word search.

fair	stair	chair
hairy	airy	dairy
pair	repair	despair
pushchair	dare	scare
beware	glare	fare
stare	care	rare
spare	mare	Belfast
Dublin	smell	stall
glass	across	buzz
dizzy	staff	stuff
yesterday	April	

o	e	c	c	y	e	s	t	e	r	d	a	y	f	r
r	i	g	z	b	e	w	a	r	e	y	h	j	f	s
l	i	z	l	h	c	p	b	l	l	s	l	d	u	f
D	i	a	c	a	y	b	u	z	z	l	t	p	t	a
d	u	a	h	g	r	r	i	b	e	e	a	a	s	i
w	r	b	x	c	t	e	i	m	r	d	h	t	r	r
e	h	y	l	u	h	t	s	a	f	l	e	B	s	e
k	a	p	a	i	e	s	d	s	r	e	r	s	m	k
f	i	a	c	r	n	r	u	i	i	c	t	s	f	
o	r	i	r	j	a	a	p	a	c	A	a	i	f	
h	y	r	o	a	n	r	m	p	p	s	p	i	d	a
z	a	h	s	h	w	e	e	e	s	s	r	r	a	t
t	l	j	s	c	a	r	e	r	e	a	i	f	i	s
k	n	z	s	m	a	r	e	a	d	l	l	x	r	s
f	z	c	e	e	i	l	k	f	o	g	v	v	y	w

Adding Endings

9. Finish the table by adding the suffixes '**s**' and '**ing**' and writing the past tense.

Remember: When adding a suffix beginning with a vowel to most words ending with '**e**', the '**e**' is dropped before adding the suffix.

Verb	Add 's'	Add 'ing'	Past tense
repair			
smell			smelt or _____
scare			
dare			

Small Words

10. Find the list or revision words that contain these small words.

(a) all _____

(b) us _____

(c) war _____

(d) me _____

Additional Activities

11. (a) Find six more homophones. Check your spelling.

(b) Write the meanings of your new sets of words.

(c) Write each of your new words in a sentence.

Unit 5

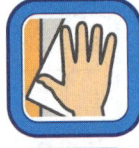

List Words	Practise	Practise	T	D
head				
breakfast				
deaf				
steady				
bread				
deadly				
lead				
tread				
instead				
ahead				
heavy				
thread				
threat				
breath				
earn				
breadth				
earl				
pearl				
death				
earth				
world				
clean				

All Mixed Up

1. Unjumble the list words.

   (a) rbtahe _____

   (b) daeha _____

   (c) srakfateb _____

   (d) tareth _____

   (e) rowdl _____

   (f) near _____

Word Challenge

2. Make as many words as you can from the word in the box. You can rearrange the letters.

   breakfast

   _____

   _____

   _____

   _____

CROSSWORD

3. Use list words to solve the crossword.

Across

1. Food baked from flour, water and yeast.
5. Obtain money in return for work.
6. The substance of the land surface.
9. _____ softly so as not to wake the baby!
10. Without hearing.
12. The distance between two sides.
15. A lord.
16. To sew you need a needle and _____.
17. Able to cause death.
19. Opposite of dirty.
20. Your neck supports this.

Down

1. The air you take in and breathe out.
2. Firmly fixed or balanced.
3. All of the people on the earth.
4. In place of something.
7. The table is too _____ to move.
8. Opposite of birth.

11. It is found in the shell of an oyster.
12. First meal of the day.
13. Further forward in space or time.
14. A statement intended to cause damage.
18. A soft, grey, heavy metal.

Shape Sorter

4. Write the list word that fits in each shape.

(a)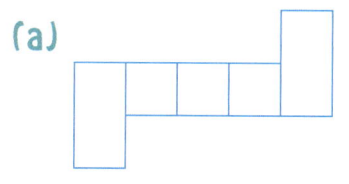

(b)

(c)

(d)

(e)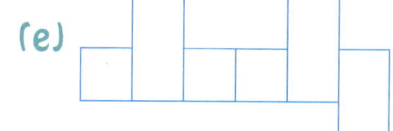

(f)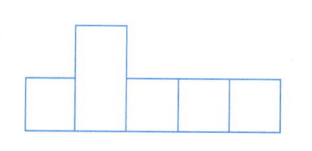

Unit 5

List Words

head
breakfast
deaf
steady
bread
deadly
lead
tread
instead
ahead
heavy
thread
threat
breath
earn
breadth
earl
pearl
death
earth
world
clean

Revision Words

riddle
ankle
eagle
bottle
little
middle
single
rectangle
part
twelve

Missing Words

5. Complete the sentences using the list or revision words.

(a) Measure the _____ of your desk in centimetres.

(b) Please serve the _____ guests their _____.

(c) The _____ of the _____ was announced in church.

(d) The old _____ pipes we lifted were very _____.

(e) The man was bitten on the _____ by a _____ snake.

Alphabetical Order

6. Write these list and revision words in alphabetical order.

thread	eagle	instead	bottle
pearl	ankle	head	middle

_____

_____

Word Meanings

7. Write the list or revision word that matches each meaning.

(a) Earth and everything on it.   _____

(b) Word puzzle.   _____

(c) Long, thin stick of graphite in a pencil.   _____

(d) Make money by working.   _____

(e) Only or one.   _____

(f) Sign of something bad.   _____

Short 'e' sound — ea

WORD SEARCH

8. Find the list and revision words in the word search.

head	instead	earl
breakfast	ahead	pearl
deaf	heavy	death
steady	thread	earth
bread	threat	world
deadly	breath	clean
lead	earn	tread
breadth	riddle	ankle
eagle	bottle	little
middle	single	
part	twelve	
rectangle		

```
s h c l e a n m i d d l e g h
d e a f p t s a f k a e r b s
h a d a c t i n s t e a d r x
e d r t e b o b e l f u m e e
a t u a w t r j l a r r g a e
v g d a h e h e g g h a m t l
y y x t a t l r a p s e e h g
a n a d x t r v e d u y a a n
r e t c h x x a e a l e a d a
d h l r m p r r e n d t l u t
u a e t l n e c z k t w i g c
c a e b t v q a x l k k u g e
t b v r j i e j r e l d d i r
m l b o t t l e e l g n i s l
d l r o w d e a d l y m n l o
```

Word Thread

9. Cross out every second letter.
The leftover letters will make three list or revision words.

_____ _____ _____

whokrmlfdsrhebcntdagnsgploepcslnehalne

Syllable Match

10. Match the syllables to make a list or revision word.

(a) in • • kle

(b) bot • • dle

(c) mid • • ly

(d) break • • tle

(e) an • • stead

(f) dead • • dle

(g) rid • • gle

(h) sin • • fast

Additional Activities

11. (a) Make word shapes for four list or revision words. Give to a friend to solve.

(b) Highlight all the nouns in the word lists.

(c) Write a paragraph, using as many of these nouns as possible.

Unit 6

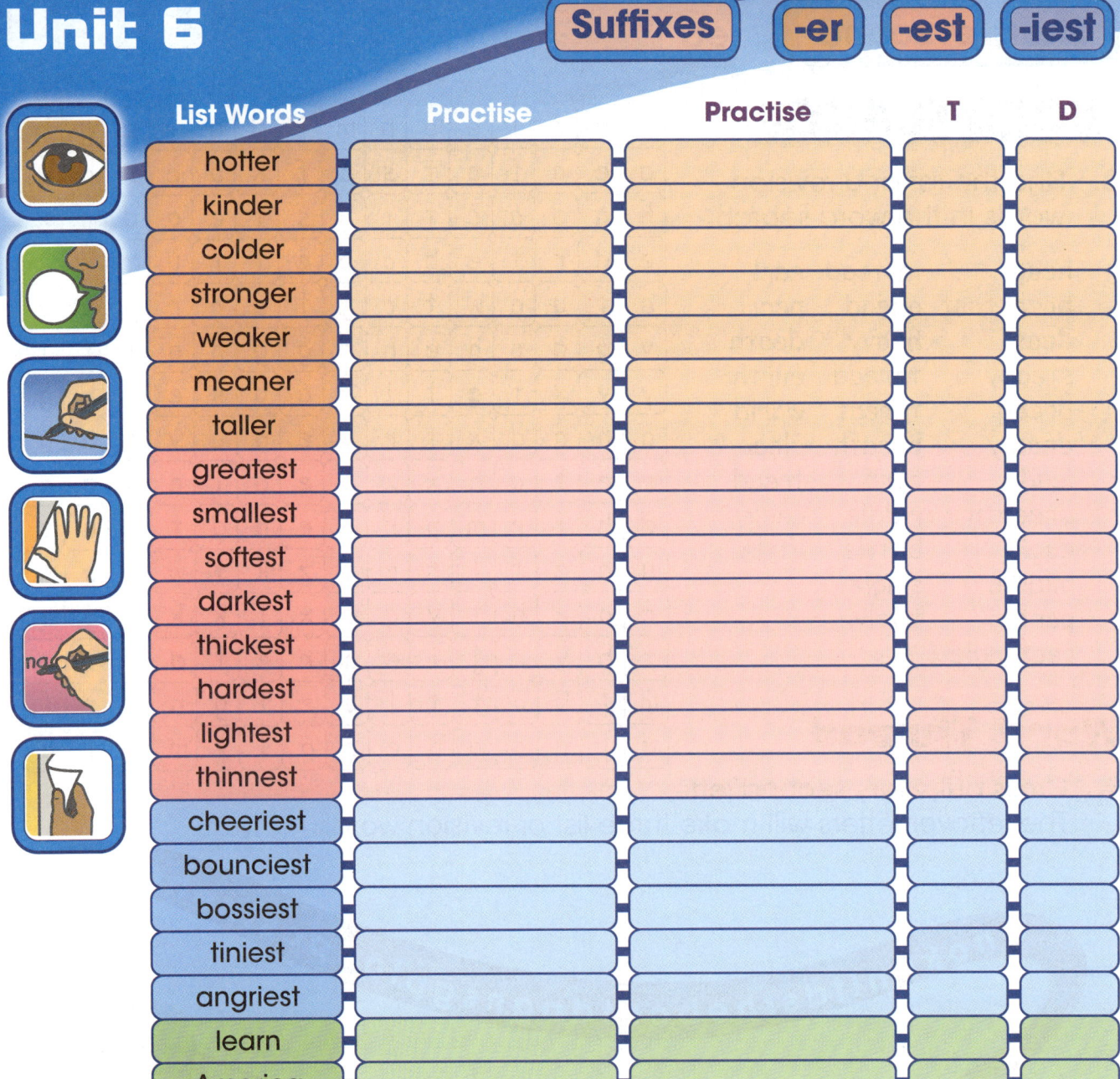

List Words	Practise	Practise	T	D
hotter				
kinder				
colder				
stronger				
weaker				
meaner				
taller				
greatest				
smallest				
softest				
darkest				
thickest				
hardest				
lightest				
thinnest				
cheeriest				
bounciest				
bossiest				
tiniest				
angriest				
learn				
America				

Comparatives

When we compare two or more people, animals or things, we usually add 'er' or 'est'; e.g. fast, faster, fastest.

For words of two or more syllables, more and most are usually used; e.g. more useful and most useful.

Some words change completely; e.g. good, better, best.

Notice how the 'y' at the end of words changes to 'i' before endings are added; e.g. pretty, prettier, prettiest.

1.

(a)		cheeriest
(b)	kinder	
(c)		lightest
(d)		bounciest
(e)	stronger	
(f)		tiniest

CROSSWORD

2. Use list words to solve the crossword.

Across

6. Largest.
7. The most firm.
9. To gain knowledge.
10. Small, smaller, _____.
13. The most furious.
15. His illness made him _____ every day.
17. The most bumpy.
18. He is five centimetres _____ than I.
19. The opposite of hardest.
20. Warmer.
21. The most slim or most lean.

Down

1. It is _____ in Iceland because of the snow.
2. USA.
3. More stingy.
4. Black is the _____ colour.
5. More powerful.
8. Happiest.

11. Weighing the least.
12. The smallest.
14. The widest, the broadest or the deepest.
16. More generous.
17. The most domineering.

Look at this word: signal
The base word for this is **sign**.

Base Words

A **base word** is a word in its simplest form.

3. Find the base word for the following words.

(a) hotter _____

(b) tiniest _____

(c) weaker _____

(d) bossiest _____

(e) lightest _____

(f) cheeriest _____

(g) darkest _____

(h) meaner _____

Unit 6

List Words

hotter
kinder
colder
stronger
weaker
meaner
taller
greatest
smallest
softest
darkest
thickest
hardest
lightest
thinnest
cheeriest
bounciest
bossiest
tiniest
angriest
learn
America

Revision Words

strap
straw
spray
sprout
sprain
screen
scream
scrape
live
usual

Missing Letters

4. Add 'er', 'est' or 'iest' to each word in brackets to complete the sentence.

   (a) (lively) The black kitten was the _____ in the litter.

   (b) (cold) It became _____ as we climbed up the mountain.

   (c) (boss) Who is the _____ manager; yours or mine?

   (d) (light) Which is the _____; the balloon, feather or rock?

Word Tail

5. Cross out every second letter. The leftover letters will make three list or revision words.

   _____ _____ _____

   secreetahmoAumseeroitcaatleecaircn

WORD HUNT

6. Which list or revision word(s) …

   (a) is an anagram of 'parts'? _____

   (b) start with the letters 'str'? _____

   _____ _____

   (c) contains the word 'ear'? _____

   (d) start with a vowel? _____

   _____

Word Challenge

7. Make as many words as you can from the word in the box. You can rearrange the letters.

   bounciest

   _____

   _____

   _____

WORD SEARCH

8. Find the list and revision words in the word search.

hotter	smallest
usual	colder
darkest	tiniest
stronger	thickest
live	weaker
hardest	learn
meaner	lightest
taller	thinnest
strap	greatest
cheeriest	straw
spray	sprout
sprain	screen
scream	scrape
angriest	bounciest
kinder	softest
bossiest	America

h	o	t	t	e	r	t	i	n	i	e	s	t	x	h	k	i
o	s	n	s	o	r	n	b	l	i	g	h	t	e	s	t	i
u	k	z	e	y	a	t	s	e	l	l	a	m	s	r	l	b
m	z	b	d	w	a	g	g	t	d	l	b	r	e	n	o	s
a	c	i	r	e	m	A	s	a	n	i	z	n	o	s	c	a
e	k	w	a	x	w	e	r	i	s	v	a	m	s	r	y	p
r	x	w	h	e	k	k	c	h	e	e	r	i	e	s	t	t
c	r	s	a	c	e	u	h	x	m	l	e	e	t	s	h	s
s	w	k	i	s	c	r	s	c	s	s	n	z	s	p	q	e
h	e	h	t	l	i	s	p	u	t	t	m	c	e	r	l	t
r	t	s	e	n	n	i	h	t	a	a	r	c	i	o	s	a
f	i	a	p	g	w	z	l	k	v	l	s	o	c	u	o	e
d	r	s	s	p	r	a	i	n	o	l	t	l	n	t	f	r
n	k	p	m	d	j	n	x	p	n	e	r	d	u	g	t	g
w	a	r	t	s	d	z	o	w	j	r	a	e	o	o	e	o
m	j	a	h	e	s	c	r	a	p	e	p	r	b	a	s	r
g	f	y	r	k	a	n	g	r	i	e	s	t	k	e	t	f

Alphabetical Order

9. Write these list and revision words in alphabetical order.

spray   darkest   screen   kinder   lightest   usual   learn   hardest

_____

_____

All Mixed Up

10. Unjumble these list and revision words.

(a) enrmae _____

(b) sulua _____

(c) fsestot _____

(d) akrsedt _____

(e) tetinsi _____

(f) cermas _____

Additional Activities

11. (a) Find and write five more comparative words. Check your spelling.

(b) Write sentences using the sets of words you have found.

(c) Write one sentence that uses as many of your new words as possible.

Unit 7

Christmas

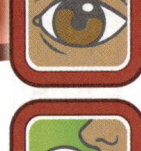

List Words	Practise	Practise	T	D
snow				
gift				
family				
chimney				
tinsel				
snowman				
party				
winter				
elves				
candles				
frost				
angel				
stable				
concert				
reindeer				
birth				
jingle				
crowds				
holy				
jolly				
ours				
theirs				

Singular and Plural

1. Complete the table.

Singular	Plural
(a)	crowds
(b)	elves
(c) party	
(d) family	
(e) snowman	
(f)	candles

Small Words

2. Find small words in these list words.

(a) theirs ________ ________ ________

(b) chimney ________

(c) concert ________ ________

(d) gift ________

(e) reindeer ________ ________ ________

(f) snow ________ ________

(g) family ________

CROSSWORD

3. Use list words to solve the crossword.

Across

2. Opposite of death.
4. You light these.
5. Short, catchy tune.
8. She sang like an _____.
10. Coldest season.
11. Sacred.
13. Belonging to them.
17. Made from snow.
18. There were _____ of people at the Christmas sale.
19. I will be with my _____ on Christmas Day.
20. Santa's helpers.

Down

1. Smoke comes out of this.
3. This animal has antlers.
4. We sang lots of carols at the school _____.
6. Happy, cheerful.
7. Everybody is invited to the Christmas _____.
9. A present.
12. We invited a friend of _____ from another school.
14. A place horses are kept.
15. Ice crystal flakes.
16. Glittering material.
19. On a cold morning you can see the _____ on the ground.

Letters into Words

4. Write three list words using the letters on the Christmas stocking. (Letters can be used more than once.)

_____

_____

_____

f, o,
v, f,
e, l,
r, s,
i, n

Shape Sorter

5. Write the word that fits in each shape.

(a)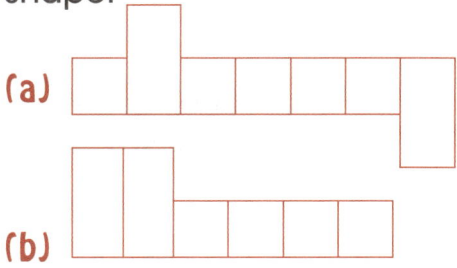

(b)

(c)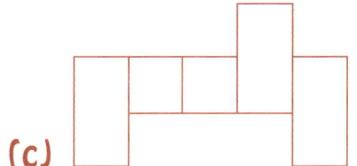

List Words

- snow
- gift
- family
- chimney
- tinsel
- snowman
- party
- winter
- elves
- candles
- frost
- angel
- stable
- concert
- reindeer
- birth
- jingle
- crowds
- holy
- jolly
- ours
- theirs

Revision Words

- snowflakes
- Advent
- December
- stocking
- holiday
- cracker
- Jesus
- Christmas
- month
- minute

Picture Story

6. Rewrite the story. Replace each picture with a list or revision word.

The  looked at the display. There was

an  above the  , a  on

_____

the roof, a  , and  with a

_____

 in the garden.

_____

Rhyming Words

7. Write a rhyming word from the list and revision words.

(a) holly _____ (b) cable _____

(c) shelves _____ (d) remember _____

(e) shocking _____ (f) lost _____

(g) sandals _____ (h) slow _____

Synonyms

8. Write list or revision words with similar meanings.

(a) cheerful _____ (b) sacred _____

(c) performance _____ (d) ice _____

(e) cherub _____ (f) present _____

WORD SEARCH

9. Find the list and revision words in the word search.

snow
chimney
party
candles
stable
jingle
ours
cracker
month
crowds
Christmas
reindeer
December

gift
tinsel
winter
frost
concert
holy
theirs
Jesus
minute
holiday
snowflakes
stocking
Advent

family
snowman
elves
angel
birth
jolly

```
                    e
              z  j  s  w  b
           o  o  c  n  g  i  e
        g  i  f  t  o  n  r  u  g
              s  J  w  i  t
           r  e  w  f  k  h  s
        u  s  p  i  l  c  C  j  o
     o  u  r  r  n  a  o  h  D  c  r
  w  s  e  e  m  t  k  t  r  e  h  j  f
why     k  l  y  e  e  s  i  c  i
     c  j  i  v  r  s  m  s  e  m  h
  a  p  p  k  f  e  o  l  t  m  n  d  o
r  l  i  r  y  f  n  s  s  m  b  e  q  l  l
c  o  n  c  e  r  t  t  r  a  e  y  e  j  y  y
  y  c  e  h  d  l  a  i  s  r  s  l  f
  c  a  n  d  l  e  s  b  e  e  n  d  x  e  c
  a  d  o  k  n  d  p  e  l  h  i  y  l  i  m  a  f
w  o  x  l  l  i  v  w  g  e  t  a  c  r  o  w  d  s  u
w  o  n  s  l  e  g  n  a  e  d  j  n  a  m  w  o  n  s
     y  r  i  s  m  i  n  u  t  e  m
     j  o  l  l  y  i  c  d  i
     q  f  o  A  d  v  e  n  t
     h  p  a  r  t  y  a
```

Secret Code

10. Use the secret code to find out the Christmas message.

11	15	8	8		1

3	12	1	3	7	4	12	1	14

3	5	12	6	13	14	9	1	13

a	1
b	2
c	3
e	4
h	5
i	6
k	7
l	8
m	9
n	10
p	11
r	12
s	13
t	14
u	15

Additional Activities

11. **(a)** Write ten more Christmas words.

(b) Write a Christmas card to your friend.

(c) Write his or her name and address on an envelope. Check with your friend if it's correct.

Unit 8

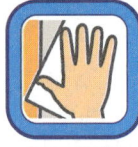

List Words	Practise	Practise	T	D
true				
value				
argue				
cue				
avenue				
screw				
flew				
brew				
dew				
drew				
igloo				
bamboo				
proof				
shampoo				
kangaroo				
fruit				
juice				
juicy				
bruise				
suit				
millimetre				
centilitre				

Missing Letters

1. Use 'ue', 'ew', 'oo', or 'ui' to complete each list word.

   (a) igl_____   (b) j_____ce

   (c) val_____   (d) s_____t

   (e) fl_____   (f) pr_____f

   (g) aven_____   (h) fr_____t

   (i) kangar_____   (j) arg_____

Small Words

2. Write the list words that contain these small words.

   (a) ice _____

   (b) me _____

   (c) of _____

   (d) am _____ _____

   (e) it _____ _____
   _____

   (f) is _____

My Spelling Workbook D—Prim-Ed Publishing—www.prim-ed.com

CROSSWORD

3. Use list words to solve the crossword.

Across

4. To make tea by mixing it with hot water.

5. To disagree or quarrel.

6. Drops of water that form on the ground during the night.

7. A liquid for washing hair.

9. Full of juice.

11. The Inuit people build this house using snow.

13. The past tense of 'fly'.

15. A broad road usually lined by trees.

17. Opposite of false.

18. Evidence or confirmation.

19. One-hundredth of a litre.

Down

1. The past tense of draw.

2. The strong, hollow stems of a tropical plant.

3. A bolt, pin or fastener for holding things together.

4. A purple mark on the skin.

8. One-thousandth of a metre.

9. The liquid that is in fruit or vegetables.

10. A large jumping marsupial from Australia.

12. A signal to an actor to start.

13. A banana, an orange, an apple or a pear.

14. The amount of money that something is worth.

16. A jacket and trousers of the same material.

Prefixes

A **prefix** is a letter or group of letters that is added to the beginning of a word to make a new word; e.g. '**milli**', meaning one-thousandth and '**centi**', meaning one-hundredth.

4. Add '**milli**' and '**centi**' to these words to make new words.

(a) centi

_____ litre

_____ metre

_____ pede

(b) milli

_____ litre

_____ metre

_____ pede

ue **ew** **oo** **ui**

List Words

true
value
argue
cue
avenue
screw
flew
brew
dew
drew
igloo
bamboo
proof
shampoo
kangaroo
fruit
juice
juicy
bruise
suit
millimetre
centilitre

Revision Words

liquid
quiet
quite
question
squeak
squash
squirm
square
oil
during

Mixed-up Sentences

5. Unjumble the sentences.

(a) good of That is value. shampoo bottle

_____

(b) A is metre. a thousandth of millimetre a

_____

(c) it bruise The had was juicy a peach on but it.

_____

_____

(d) lot questions were kangaroo. about missing There a of the quite

_____

_____

Tenses

6. Complete the table by writing the correct tense; e.g. grow, grows, grew.

	Verb	Add 's'	Add 'ing'	Past tense
(a)				drew
(b)				flew
(c)	argue			
(d)	squeak			
(e)	squash			

Secret Code

7. Use the secret code to find out the list or revision words.

a	b	c	d	g	h	i	k	l	m	n	o	p	q	r	s	t	u
1	2	3	4	5	6	7	8	9	10	11	12	13	14	15	16	17	18

(a) _ _ _ _ _ _
    2 1 10 2 12 12

(b) _ _ _ _ _ _   (c) _ _ _ _ _
    4 18 15 7 11 5   7 5 9 12 12

WORD SEARCH

8. Find the list and revision words in the word search.

true	dew	juice
value	drew	juicy
argue	igloo	bruise
cue	bamboo	suit
avenue	proof	screw
flew	kangaroo	brew
fruit	liquid	quiet
quite	question	squeak
squash	squirm	square
oil	during	shampoo
millimetre		centilitre

x	q	u	e	s	t	i	o	n	k	e	r	a	u	q	s
n	e	i	j	q	q	x	o	w	m	h	s	b	d	s	x
s	q	u	a	s	h	r	r	e	a	d	e	t	i	u	q
j	v	h	n	a	g	e	a	r	e	m	r	i	u	q	s
u	t	y	w	e	x	o	g	c	p	g	j	c	q	u	e
i	o	i	e	y	v	u	n	s	i	j	u	l	i	o	r
c	c	o	u	s	e	a	a	l	d	k	i	t	l	c	t
e	j	k	p	r	i	j	k	u	x	t	c	i	c	p	e
r	y	h	d	m	f	u	r	g	r	r	y	x	k	e	m
y	l	r	z	s	a	i	r	m	q	u	d	g	w	u	i
t	e	i	u	q	n	h	f	b	o	e	v	e	o	l	l
w	r	z	b	g	r	l	s	r	o	k	r	u	o	a	l
l	a	s	q	u	e	a	k	s	l	b	z	c	b	v	i
q	i	r	w	w	d	n	p	m	g	v	t	r	m	w	m
p	z	i	c	e	n	t	i	l	i	t	r	e	a	h	x
v	u	c	u	e	d	t	g	p	r	o	o	f	b	e	p

Synonyms

9. Write list or revision words with similar meanings.

(a) factual _____

(b) worth _____

(c) quarrel _____

(d) outfit _____

(e) prompt _____

(f) wriggle _____

(g) evidence _____

(h) squeal _____

Antonyms

10. Write list or revision words with opposite meanings.

(a) false _____

(b) loud _____

(c) agree _____

(d) dry _____

(e) solid _____

(f) answer _____

Additional Activities

11. (a) Find five more 'centi' and 'milli' words.

(b) Write sentences using your new words.

(c) Write your new words in alphabetical order.

Unit 9

List Words	Practise	Practise	T	D
parcel				
since				
certain				
century				
centipede				
prince				
acid				
calcium				
cigar				
circuit				
pencil				
stencil				
cinema				
circle				
circumference				
cylinder				
cycle				
cyclone				
cymbal				
agency				
found				
study				

Missing Letters

1. Use 'ce', 'ci' or 'cy' to complete each list word.

(a) sten____ ____l

(b) ____ ____ cle

(c) sin____ ____

(d) ____ ____ nema

(e) ____ ____ linder

(f) ____ ____ rcuit

(g) ____ ____rcumference

(h) par____ ____l

(i) a____ ____d

(j) ____ ____ntipede

(k) prin____ ____

(l) pen____ ____l

More Than One

To make plurals of nouns ending in 'y' following a consonant, change the 'y' to 'i' and add 'es'; e.g. baby – babies.

2. Make these words plural, following the rule where necessary.

(a) century _____

(b) cymbal _____

(c) agency _____

(d) study _____

(e) cyclone _____

CROSSWORD

3. Use list words to solve the crossword.

Across

1. A round brass musical instrument.
2. To write you need a pen or a _____.
6. One hundred years.
8. We booked our holidays in a travel _____.
9. I often _____ to school.
11. Sharp-tasting or sour.
14. A circular line or route.
16. It is easy to draw something using a _____.
17. Windstorm, gale or hurricane.
18. The distance around something.

Down

1. Sure or positive.
2. It is often wrapped in paper and sent by post.
3. A theatre where films are shown.
4. A room for reading, writing or working.
5. The past tense of 'find'.
7. A creature with many legs and a long body.
10. In the old films, men often smoke a _____.
12. The son of a king or queen.
13. A 3-D shape with three surfaces.
14. A soft, white element found in bones and teeth.
15. A ring.
16. During or in the time after.

Proofreading

When the letter 'c' is followed by an 'e', 'i' or 'y', it has a soft 'c' sound.

4. Circle the incorrect words and rewrite the sentence on the line below.

(a) The prinse wanted to smoke a sigar in the sinema.

_____

(b) I am sertain there is a sentipede in that parsel.

_____

(c) The asid in fizzy drinks attacks the calsium in your teeth.

_____

Unit 9

List Words

parcel
since
certain
century
centipede
prince
acid
calcium
cigar
circuit
pencil
stencil
cinema
circle
circumference
cylinder
cycle
cyclone
cymbal
agency
found
study

Revision Words

told
folder
scold
older
remind
kindest
behind
blind
again
name

Word Hunt

5. Which list or revision word(s) …

(a) has the most letters? _____

(b) can be a verb and a noun?

_____

_____

_____

Word Challenge

6. Make as many words as you can from the word in the box. You can rearrange the letters.

circumference

_____

_____

Describing Words

7. Write the correct noun from the list or revision words. Draw the pictures these adjectives describe.

(a) creepy, small

(b) royal, handsome

Synonyms

8. Write list or revision words with similar meanings.

(a) package _____ (b) tell off _____

(c) ring _____ (d) sightless _____

(e) learn _____ (f) sure _____

(g) file _____ (h) track _____

WORD SEARCH

9. Find the list and revision words in the word search.

parcel   cigar   told
cyclone   folder   study
cycle   since   acid
circuit   again   older
certain   pencil   scold
name   century
stencil   kindest
cinema   found
cylinder   remind
blind   prince
circle   agency
calcium   behind
cymbal   centipede
circumference

u	o	c	o	e	c	n	e	e	d	e	p	i	t	n	e	c	h
m	i	z	i	g	q	o	l	d	e	r	e	l	c	r	i	c	d
h	u	n	a	r	g	p	c	a	w	t	s	b	b	u	s	e	n
d	g	i	b	i	c	v	v	c	y	c	l	o	n	e	d	f	u
f	u	a	c	l	x	u	r	w	i	e	n	k	m	x	w	v	o
c	p	g	n	l	i	i	m	v	s	x	t	r	a	g	i	c	f
y	e	a	i	x	a	n	c	f	y	s	f	p	e	n	c	i	l
p	p	n	a	y	s	c	d	f	e	c	f	p	r	i	z	y	g
a	f	j	t	d	d	p	b	d	a	r	v	b	n	i	o	t	n
r	r	a	r	u	l	b	n	v	l	y	e	e	e	g	n	d	j
c	e	l	e	t	r	i	e	r	w	y	m	n	j	q	j	c	a
e	d	a	c	s	k	y	e	h	t	a	y	n	c	s	t	s	e
l	l	b	t	q	e	m	c	e	i	o	a	k	b	e	i	t	r
h	o	m	f	v	i	d	t	g	e	n	l	l	s	x	u	e	k
d	f	y	w	n	u	e	c	n	i	s	d	d	c	a	c	n	n
g	i	c	d	y	e	l	c	y	c	x	l	f	o	c	r	c	a
p	a	c	n	d	j	v	a	g	e	n	c	y	l	y	i	i	m
c	s	q	a	u	r	e	d	n	i	l	y	c	d	v	c	l	e

Syllable Match

10. Match the syllables to make list or revision words.

(a) be • • der _____

(b) prin • • er _____

(c) fold • • cle _____

(d) ac • • hind _____

(e) ol • • id _____

(f) cir • • ce _____

(g) cir • • mind _____

(h) re • • cuit _____

Changing Words

11. Change one letter in each word to make a list or revision word.

(a) came _____

(b) round _____

(c) blink _____

(d) prance _____

(e) arid _____

(f) cold _____

Additional Activities

12. (a) Write six more 'ce', 'ci' or 'cy' words.

   (b) Use a dictionary to write a definition for each of your new words.

   (c) Write a paragraph that includes all six of your new words.

Unit 10

List Words	Practise	Practise	T	D
didn't				
haven't				
couldn't				
wouldn't				
shouldn't				
can't				
wasn't				
aren't				
we'd				
doesn't				
they'll				
let's				
who'd				
who's				
brother-in-law				
passer-by				
hanger-on				
by-law				
drive-in				
take-off				
Europe				
great				

Contractions

There are two main uses for apostrophes. One is to show when a letter or letters have been omitted.

1. Write the contraction for these:

   (a) who would _____

   (b) they will _____

   (c) let us _____

   (d) are not _____

   (e) could not _____

Hyphenated Words

Hyphenated words are compound words that would be unclear, hard to read or excessively long without the hyphen; e.g. *no-smoking sign* and *black-cab driver.*

2. Rewrite these words, putting in the hyphens.

   (a) passerby _____

   (b) brotherinlaw _____

   (c) drivein _____

   (d) bylaw _____

CROSSWORD

3. Use list words to solve the crossword.

Across

4. Short for 'could not'.

8. Short for 'we would', 'we should' or 'we had'.

9. A person who goes past something.

10. Short for 'let us'.

12. Short for 'was not'.

15. Short for 'who had' or 'who would'.

17. The husband of one's sister.

18. Short for 'they shall' or 'they will'.

19. Short for 'does not'.

20. A person who follows or stays around someone.

Down

1. Short for 'cannot'.

2. The second smallest continent.

3. Large, big, or huge.

5. Short for 'did not'.

6. Short for 'are not'.

7. A rule made by the local authority.

8. Short for 'who is' or 'who has'.

11. Short for 'have not'.

12. Short for 'would not'.

13. The plane was ready to _____ at two.

14. Short for 'should not'.

16. A restaurant or cinema you can visit without leaving your car.

Apostrophe

4. Put the apostrophe in the correct place. Use a coloured pencil.

(a) wasnt _____

(b) shouldnt _____

(c) havent _____

(d) whos _____

Shape Sorter

5. Write the word that fits in each shape.

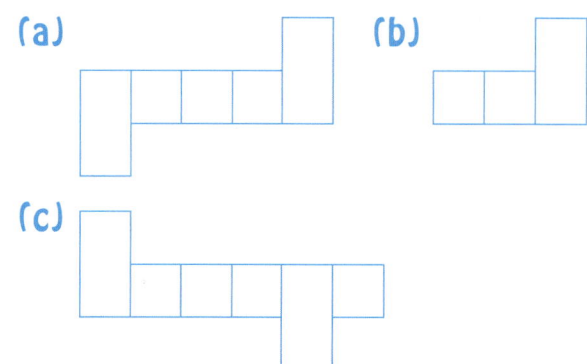

(a)

(b)

(c)

Unit 10   Contractions   Hyphenated Words

List Words

didn't
haven't
couldn't
wouldn't
shouldn't
can't
wasn't
aren't
we'd
doesn't
they'll
let's
who'd
who's
brother-in-law
passer-by
hanger-on
by-law
drive-in
take-off
Europe
great

Revision Words

race
space
trace
disgrace
price
ice-cream
voice
advice
January
because

Missing Words

6. Complete the sentences using the list or revision words.

(a) _____ go to the cafe for an _____.

(b) The police gave us _____ on the traffic _____.

(c) I _____ got a passport to go to _____.

(d) I think it would be _____ to go into _____ in a rocket.

Proofreading

7. Circle the incorrect words and rewrite them correctly in the spaces.

(a) I can't believe the prise of that isecream.

_____   _____

(b) There is no trase of the passerby who saw the crash.

_____   _____

(c) We coulndt go to that drivein for burgers becos it has closed down.

_____   _____   _____

Compound Words

8. Match the words to make hyphenated compound words.

(a) ice   •   • off   _____

(b) take   •   • law   _____

(c) drive   •   • cream   _____

(d) passer   •   • on   _____

(e) hanger   •   • by   _____

(f) by   •   • in   _____

WORD SEARCH

9. Find the list and revision words in the word search.

didn't	Europe
haven't	doesn't
by-law	take-off
couldn't	they'll
drive-in	wouldn't
let's	shouldn't
who'd	we'd
can't	who's
great	wasn't
race	aren't
passer-by	trace
disgrace	price
voice	advice
January	because
ice-cream	space
brother-in-law	
hanger-on	

```
t h e y l l v e t y f d n b t t b
t w o u l d n t a g t o e w m n n
e l p e s t b q e q r c y w a s d
i e t o b v h c r e a z r k e e c
f s h y p p r f g u g r a r r o w
o w a l y b f n s d n s u d c d a
d y i g s o a e m i g n n p e g a
p o h r e h e g u s e t a p c k d
e i h k o a c o u g c n J a i p r
t c a w d v a z d r i e e s f e i
i t a q t e r w c a v r c s h c v
a n m r n n t t a c d a i e g i e
l s m w d t m s n e a h r r f o i
w a l n i r e h t o r b p b l v n
r w t q d x e p o r u E h y q x r
i t n d l u o h s x f t m r k y k
s m k t n d l u o c s p a c e g h
```

Word Alien

10. Cross out every second letter to make three list or revision words.

_____ _____ _____

sthlofuglsdbnc'tgEyuprrotpnewbcekclapurswep

More Than One

Some **compound nouns** add 's' to the first word; others add 's' to the second word; e.g. chief-of-staff — chiefs-of-staff, lay-by — lay-bys.

11. Make these words plural. Use a dictionary.

(a) drive-in _____

(b) brother-in-law _____

(c) ice-cream _____

(d) take-off _____

(e) passer-by _____

(f) by-law _____

Additional Activities

12. (a) Write five contraction words. Check your spelling.

(b) Write five more hyphenated words.

(c) Write sentences, with each sentence containing a contraction word and a hyphenated word.

Unit 11

List Words	Practise	Practise	T	D
people				
angle				
vegetable				
simple				
terrible				
puzzle				
agile				
axle				
sprinkle				
assemble				
travel				
angel				
label				
level				
towel				
tunnel				
novel				
jewel				
fuel				
cancel				
kilogram				
kilometre				

Syllable Match

1. Match the syllables and write the list words.

    (a) tra • • kle _____

    (b) an • • ple _____

    (c) sprin • • gle _____

    (d) sim • • vel _____

    (e) an • • bel _____

    (f) la • • gel _____

Missing Letters

2. Use 'le' or 'el' to complete the list words.

    (a) tunn___ ___

    (b) assemb___ ___

    (c) fu___ ___

    (d) agi___ ___

    (e) vegetab___ ___

    (f) canc___ ___

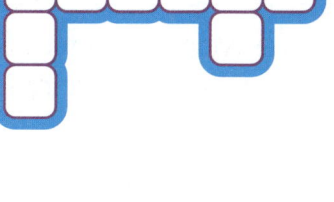
CROSSWORD

3. Use list words to solve the crossword.

Across

1. To make a journey.
5. A source of energy.
7. 1000 metres.
8. Awful or dreadful.
9. A messenger of God.
11. A rod that passes through the centre of a wheel.
12. To gather together.
15. Active, fit and supple.
16. A precious stone.
18. A book with an invented story.
19. You need patience to finish a jigsaw _____.
20. To call off.

Down

1. Used for drying one's body.
2. Potato, carrot or cabbage.
3. An underground passage.
4. 1000 grams.
6. Identification tag.
10. Easy.
11. The Tower in Pisa leans at a 20 degree _____.
13. To scatter small drops.
14. Human beings.
17. Flat, smooth or even.

Adding Endings

4. When a word ends in a single 'l', double the 'l' when a suffix beginning with a vowel is added; e.g. pedal – pedalled – pedalling.

	Verb	Add 's'	Add 'ing'	Past tense
(a)	travel			
(b)	label			
(c)	cancel			
(d)	sprinkle			
(e)	assemble			
(f)	tunnel			

Unit 11

List Words

people
angle
vegetable
simple
terrible
puzzle
agile
axle
sprinkle
assemble
travel
angel
label
level
towel
tunnel
novel
jewel
fuel
cancel
kilogram
kilometre

Revision Words

huge
stage
bridge
judge
branch
crunch
match
catch
please
February

Alphabetical Order

5. Write these list and revision words in alphabetical order.

kilometre   crunch   travel   fuel

February   cancel   huge   judge

_____

_____

Mixed-up Sentences

6. Unjumble the sentences.

(a) get people work. to travel Some through the prefer tunnel go over to the than bridge to

_____

_____

(b) is hospital. terrible have that It due fresh for the crunch we cancel credit the of vegetables to the to order

_____

_____

_____

Rhyming Words

7. Write a rhyming word from the list and revision words.

(a) fudge _____   **(b)** funnel _____

(c) wrinkle _____   **(d)** guzzle _____

(e) pimple _____   **(f)** tease _____

(g) table _____   **(h)** hunch _____

WORD SEARCH

8. Find the list and revision words in the word search.

people	sprinkle	novel
angle	branch	jewel
travel	fuel	simple
angel	cancel	label
puzzle	level	crunch
please	agile	catch
towel	huge	bridge
axle	tunnel	
stage	kilometre	
judge	assemble	
terrible	vegetable	
kilogram	February	

f	e	f	b	l	s	k	e	u	t	o	w	e	l	d	a	r
m	l	b	c	e	s	e	g	k	b	c	a	n	c	e	l	s
a	b	l	s	g	q	l	a	k	r	j	z	u	j	l	t	y
r	m	e	j	n	m	z	t	r	a	v	e	l	q	a	r	r
g	e	n	i	a	t	z	s	k	n	l	d	y	b	w	u	a
o	s	n	j	b	k	u	w	o	c	u	e	l	h	j	l	u
l	s	u	s	i	m	p	l	e	h	l	e	b	d	s	e	r
i	a	t	i	v	b	p	l	n	r	g	e	r	a	o	w	b
k	t	l	k	i	l	o	m	e	t	r	e	v	l	l	e	e
e	l	i	g	a	y	v	a	o	a	v	c	e	e	i	j	F
k	t	t	e	r	r	i	b	l	e	s	v	g	u	l	x	j
e	l	g	n	a	x	b	r	z	w	o	e	e	f	a	w	p
c	r	u	n	c	h	e	i	l	n	h	c	t	a	c	h	e
s	w	e	b	q	j	u	d	g	e	e	s	a	m	w	s	g
p	e	o	p	l	e	z	g	q	t	l	j	b	u	d	v	u
t	k	r	d	u	h	b	e	t	g	x	n	l	v	r	c	h
r	v	s	p	r	i	n	k	l	e	a	s	e	y	p	b	u

Synonyms

9. Write list or revision words with similar meanings.

(a) call off _____

(b) nimble _____

(c) give your opinion _____

(d) precious stone _____

(e) steady _____

(f) awful _____

(g) 1000 grams _____

(h) burrow _____

10. Use the secret code to find out the list or revision words.

a	d	e	g	h	j	l	s	t	u	w	x
1	2	3	4	5	6	7	8	9	10	11	12

(a) __ __ __ __
   1 12 7 3

(b) __ __ __ __ __
   8 9 1 4 3

(c) __ __ __ __
   5 10 4 3

(d) __ __ __ __ __
   6 3 11 3 7

Additional Activities

11. (a) Write ten more mathematical words. Check your spelling.

(b) Write your ten words in alphabetical order.

(c) Write a definition for each of your ten words.

Unit 12

List Words	Practise	Practise	T	D
outdoor				
outline				
outbreak				
outfit				
outcry				
undo				
untie				
uneven				
unable				
unaware				
overboard				
overcast				
overhead				
overall				
overbook				
underage				
underground				
understand				
undercover				
underneath				
Edinburgh				
London				

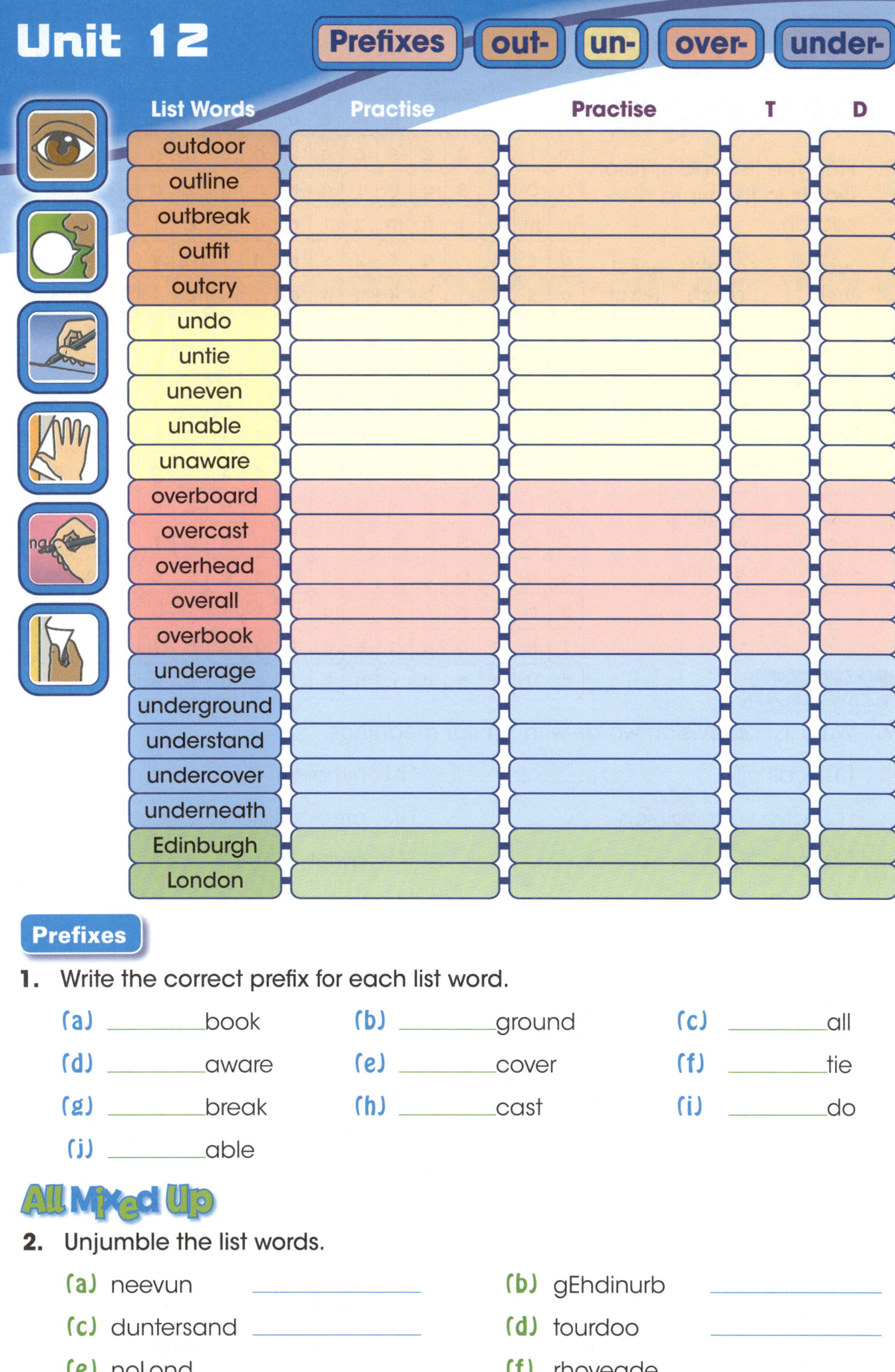

Prefixes

1. Write the correct prefix for each list word.

(a) _____book   (b) _____ground   (c) _____all

(d) _____aware   (e) _____cover   (f) _____tie

(g) _____break   (h) _____cast   (i) _____do

(j) _____able

All Mixed Up

2. Unjumble the list words.

(a) neevun _____   (b) gEhdinurb _____

(c) duntersand _____   (d) tourdoo _____

(e) noLond _____   (f) rhoveade _____

CROSSWORD

3. Use list words to solve the crossword.

Across

2. Capital of the United Kingdom.

4. We tried to _____ the knot in the string.

6. Lacking the skill to do something.

7. To comprehend.

9. Below the legal or required age for something.

11. To accept more reservations than there is room for.

13. My mum got a new _____ to go to the wedding.

14. From a ship into the water.

17. Opposite of 'above'.

19. Cloudy or dull weather.

20. Capital of Scotland.

Down

1. Not level or smooth.

3. Having no knowledge of a fact or situation.

5. There was an _____ of chicken pox in our school.

6. Opposite of 'above ground'.

8. Involving secret work to obtain information.

10. A strong expression of public disapproval.

11. A line indicating the shape of an object.

12. In the sky or above one's head.

15. Opposite of 'indoor'.

16. Taking everything into account.

18. Undo knot in something.

Prefixes

4. Write the correct prefix next to its meaning. Choose two list words as examples.

Prefix	Meaning	List Words	
(a)	below, beneath		
(b)	not, the opposite		
(c)	beyond, too much		
(d)	outside, beyond the limit		

Unit 12

List Words

outdoor
outline
outbreak
outfit
outcry
undo
untie
uneven
unable
unaware
overboard
overcast
overhead
overall
overbook
underage
underground
understand
undercover
underneath
Edinburgh
London

Compound Words

5. Make compound words from these list and revision words.

(a) some •   • book   (b) every •   • self
    over •   • side   under •   • side
    under •   • times   my   •   • where
    sea   •   • cover   off   •   • age

Missing Words

6. Complete the sentences using the list or revision words.

(a) The English workers in _____ could not

_____ the Scottish workers in _____.

(b) _____ was disappointed that the trip to

the _____ was cancelled as the weather

was so _____.

(c) The captain thought that _____ had

fallen _____ but we were _____

to find them.

---

yourself
myself
offside
seaside
someone
sometimes
everyone
everywhere
oil
metre

Word Raft

7. Cross out every second letter. The left-over letters will make three list or revision words.

_____   _____   _____

o b v g e d r t a k l e l p o w i m l f y a o f u h r l s n e p l r f

WORD SEARCH

. Find the list and revision words in the word search.

outdoor	outline
outbreak	outfit
outcry	undo
untie	uneven
unable	unaware
overboard	overcast
overhead	overall
overbook	everywhere
underground	everyone
undercover	underage
Edinburgh	London
yourself	myself
offside	seaside
someone	sometimes
understand	metre
underneath	oil

```
s e m i t e m o s f l l a r e v o
h u h x y j f l e s r u o y o s u
g n g j x o e o n e w o u t f i t
a e r o d u u v o o u t l i n e d
u v u a o t n e e v e w v i o r b
n e b d t d d r m r e i a f a e a
d n n e o o e h o o y r t o a r o
e u i d f o r e s u e w b n L t v
r n d i f r a a u v t r h o u e e
n e E s s l g d o n e b n e o m r
e v k a i x e c a v a d r m r k c
a e k e d m r s o o o w t e o e a
t r k s e e t x y n u c a s a b s
h y s a d e c v v m v t q r v k t
r o y n u n a b l e a z c h e x p
q n u n d e r g r o u n d r o i l
k e f d n a t s r e d n u m y z m
```

Synonyms

9. Write list or revision words with similar meanings.

(a) epidemic _____　　(b) cloudy _____

(c) secretly _____　　(d) grease _____

(e) ignorant _____　　(f) protest _____

(g) occasionally _____　　(h) rough _____

WORD HUNT

10. Which list or revision word(s) …

(a) ends in 'ie'? _____

(b) are capital cities? _____

_____

(c) is a unit of measurement? _____

(d) is the longest word? _____

(e) is the shortest word? _____

Additional Activities

11. (a) Write five more words with these prefixes. Check your spelling.

(b) Write your five words in alphabetical order.

(c) Write a paragraph that contains all five of your new words.

Unit 13

List Words	Practise	Practise	T	D
chick				
garden				
crown				
rabbit				
flowers				
flowerbed				
heaven				
daisy				
hatch				
rainbow				
raincoat				
tomb				
puddle				
foal				
meadow				
springtime				
windy				
daffodil				
splash				
worship				
point				
letter				

Small Words

1. Find small words in these list words.

(a) heaven _____

(b) crown _____

(c) worship _____

(d) point _____

(e) flowers _____

(f) meadow _____

Letters into Words

2. Write three list words using the letters in the puddle. (Letters can be used more than once.)

_____

_____

_____

D, S, H, W, A, I, K, N, Y, C

CROSSWORD

3. Use list words to solve the crossword.

Across

2. Baby chicken.
3. Come out of egg.
5. Colours of the …
6. Sharp end of something.
8. Small flower.
10. Grassy field.
13. Time between winter and summer.
15. A yellow flower.
17. Postman delivers this.
19. Perfect dwelling place after death.

Down

1. Used to keep the rain off.
4. A king or queen wears this on their head.
5. Animal associated with Easter.
6. A collection of water on the road.
7. Blustery.
9. Plot for plants.
11. Adoration.
12. A bouquet of …
13. Scatter liquid.
14. Cultivated area around house.
16. Baby horse.
18. Mummies are buried in this.

Shape Sorter

4. Write the word that fits in each shape.

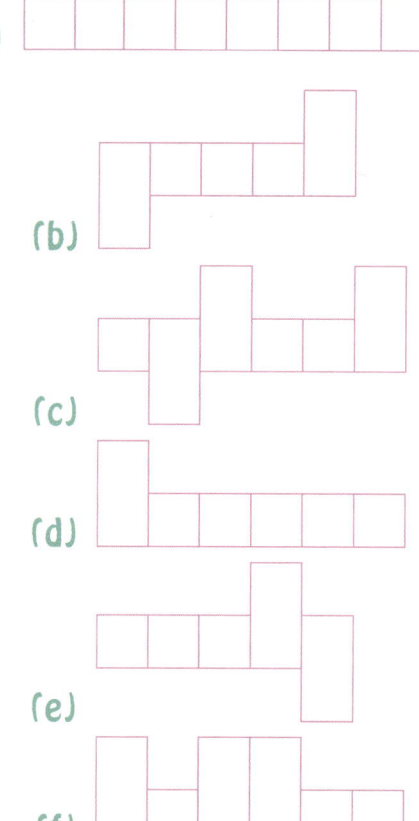

(a)

(b)

(c)

(d)

(e)

(f)

Unit 13

List Words

chick
garden
crown
rabbit
flowers
flowerbed
heaven
daisy
hatch
rainbow
raincoat
tomb
puddle
foal
meadow
springtime
windy
daffodil
splash
worship
point
letter

Revision Words

bonnet
cloud
Christ
crocus
Easter
death
dragonfly
bluebird
eighteen
seventeen

Missing Words

5. Write list or revision words in the spaces to complete the story.

The _____ hopped about in the _____.

He nibbled hungrily at a _____ and a

_____. A _____ swooped down to drink

from a _____ near him, in the

_____ of the statue that stood in the

_____.

What am I?

6. I float.
I am carried by the wind.
I range in colour from white to dark grey.
I can carry water.

I am a _____.

Compound Words

7. Make compound words from these list and revision words.

(a) rain •   • time

(b) dragon •   • bow

(c) rain •   • bed

(d) spring •   • fly

(e) flower •   • coat

Secret Code

8. Use the secret code to find out the message.

___ ___ ___ ___   ___   ___ ___ ___ ___ ___
6   1   11   3   1   6   1   7   7   12

___ ___ ___ ___ ___ ___
3   1   9   10   3   8

1	a
2	d
3	e
4	f
5	g
6	h
7	p
8	r
9	s
10	t
11	v
12	y

Spring/Easter

WORD SEARCH

9. Find the list and revision words in the word search.

chick	garden	crown
flowers	flowerbed	heaven
hatch	rainbow	raincoat
puddle	foal	meadow
windy	daffodil	splash
point	letter	bonnet
Christ	crocus	Easter
dragonfly	bluebird	eighteen
rabbit	daisy	tomb
springtime	worship	cloud
death	seventeen	

The word search grid (in the shape of a church):

```
        y
        d
      i n p
    f j i h r
  c r o w n a z
    a q a r i
    i w c l n
    n c o r c
    b l l d o
  w o o x C a c
a n w u r h t e u
r k e o d j r a p m s
x t y d c q u i w u o k v
  s r y h h s f d a
  i a g s i t o d s
  a g a g a c h l e
  d l m p u c k e v
  p r m x d e b r e w o l f d
s l e t t e r y d n f n x l r t
p e t t z h h y s f t j m n o a z r
q x m y s d h d n o t e y k h w g h y
  i e a o r p y e e e e y a e o e r
  t d E k s i n c e n u v t r n a u
  g o p e u n b h g t v m c s f v y
  n d m y o o j e w p h y h p l e k
  i m e b j w r j u w r g a r y n r
  r d t a k w b z j l o l i v e p w
  p o i n t v p t i b b a r e s f j
  s w o r s h i p b p j b x e y t x
m n h u l i d o f f a d g l m f n e x
```

Rhyming Words

10. Write a rhyming word from the list and revision words.

(a) breath _____

(b) proud _____

(c) coal _____

(d) focus _____

(e) better _____

(f) crash _____

(g) zoom _____

(h) cuddle _____

Additional Activities

11. (a) Write a list of eight activities for your Easter holiday.

(b) Write your eight activities in alphabetical order.

(c) Write an invitation to a friend, inviting him or her to join you on one of these activities.

Unit 14

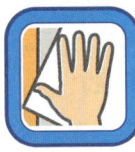

List Words	Practise	Practise	T	D
helpless				
harmless				
careless				
hopeless				
needless				
breathless				
sadness				
awareness				
sickness				
happiness				
weakness				
braveness				
cleanliness				
business				
quietly				
lonely				
wisely				
lovely				
brightly				
quickly				
kind				
engage				

Singular Words

A **suffix** is a group of letters which is added to the end of a word to form a new word; e.g. help + less = helpless.

1. Write the correct suffix to make a list word.

(a) brave + _____ = _____

(b) sad + _____ = _____

(c) bright + _____ = _____

(d) need + _____ = _____

(e) love + _____ = _____

Small Words

2. Write the list words that contain these small words.

(a) age _____

(b) is _____

(c) at _____

(d) on _____

(e) are _____

_____

(f) in _____

_____

CROSSWORD

3. Use list words to solve the crossword.

Across

1. Done badly without enough attention.
7. Knowing about.
9. The lack of physical strength and energy.
11. Good hygiene.
13. Weak or powerless.
16. Unnecessary.
18. The state of being ill.
19. My dad runs a _____ selling cars.
20. Opposite of 'slowly'.

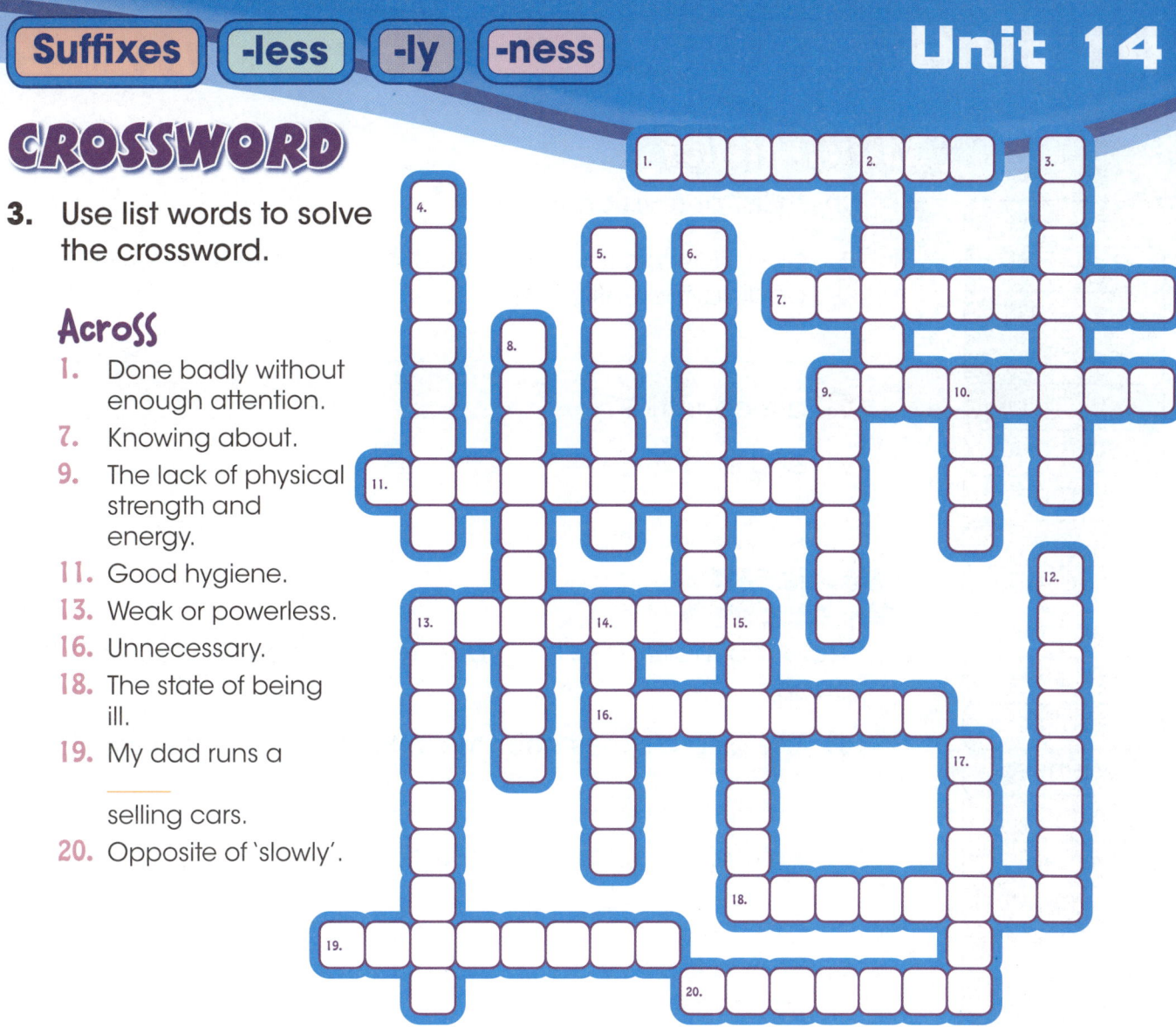

Down

2. To involve someone's interest or attention.
3. Feeling or causing despair.
4. The room was _____ lit by the sun.
5. Softly in a low tone.
6. Courage.
8. Gasping for breath.
9. Knowing much from experience.
10. Generous.
12. Not likely or able to cause harm.
13. Contentment.
14. Solitary.
15. Unhappiness.
17. Beautiful, pretty or attractive.

Suffixes

4. Write the correct suffix next to its meaning.
Choose two list words as examples.

Suffix	Meaning	List Words	
(a)	like, manner		
(b)	without		
(c)	quality or condition		

Unit 14

List Words

- helpless
- harmless
- careless
- hopeless
- needless
- breathless
- sadness
- awareness
- sickness
- happiness
- weakness
- braveness
- cleanliness
- business
- quietly
- lonely
- wisely
- lovely
- brightly
- quickly
- kind
- engage

WORD HUNT

5. Which list or revision word(s) …

(a) are following the rule – change the 'y' to 'i' before adding the suffix 'ness'?

_____   _____   _____

(b) are countries?   _____   _____

(c) end in 'd'?   _____   _____

Proofreading

6. Circle the incorrect words and rewrite them correctly in the space.

(a) Theres a bisenes near me in Scotlind that makes kilts.

_____   _____   _____

(b) Theyve completed their work queitly and qickly.

_____   _____   _____

(c) Shes a loneley but armless lady who lives in the big house.

_____   _____   _____

Revision Words

- there's
- won't
- she's
- you'll
- weren't
- they've
- you're
- hasn't
- Wales
- Scotland

Letters Into Words

7. Write four list or revision words using these letters. (Letters can be used more than once.)

_____   _____

_____   _____

WORD SEARCH

8. Find the list and revision words in the word search.

helpless
wisely
happiness
careless
brightly
braveness
needless
kind
business
sadness
there's
lonely
she's
weren't
Scotland
Wales

sickness
harmless
lovely
weakness
hopeless
quickly
cleanliness
breathless
engage
quietly
awareness
won't
you'll
they've
hasn't
you're

q	u	i	c	k	l	y	v	c	u	v	y	z	y	v	s	z
s	s	e	l	h	t	a	e	r	b	l	v	l	o	s	d	u
c	m	y	z	i	e	g	a	g	n	e	o	y	e	v	r	e
a	y	l	t	h	g	i	r	b	n	f	p	n	o	v	t	i
r	f	e	s	v	t	x	q	l	s	e	d	j	e	u	o	q
e	w	s	s	s	e	n	i	l	n	a	e	l	c	l	r	l
l	e	i	e	d	q	d	p	s	s	w	t	d	t	a	y	e
e	r	w	n	t	s	w	d	s	h	o	p	e	l	e	s	s
s	e	s	e	h	d	e	s	e	a	j	u	k	c	e	w	e
s	n	i	v	e	n	a	e	n	w	t	n	s	a	h	s	h
s	t	c	a	y	a	k	r	i	a	f	f	m	x	e	q	s
e	d	k	r	v	l	n	e	p	r	d	t	f	l	b	a	e
l	f	n	b	e	t	e	h	p	e	m	a	a	s	h	t	u
m	q	e	i	h	o	s	t	a	n	x	W	l	l	u	o	y
r	e	s	e	k	c	s	s	h	e	y	l	t	e	i	u	q
a	p	s	i	w	S	s	b	s	s	e	n	i	s	u	b	m
h	e	l	p	l	e	s	s	w	s	w	n	r	w	o	n	t

Missing Words

9. Complete the sentences using the list or revision words.

(a) _____ a _____ castle in Edinburgh, _____.

(b) The man was very _____ with his _____.

(c) The _____ old lady from _____ spoke very _____.

Antonyms

10. Find list or revision words with the opposite meanings.

(a) cruel _____

(b) will _____

(c) cowardice _____

(d) health _____

(e) slowly _____

(f) has _____

Additional Activities

11. (a) Write the list and revision words in alphabetical order. Check your spelling.

(b) Make word shapes for six of the words.

(c) Make a word worm containing three of the words.

List Words	Practise	Practise	T	D
crept				
swept				
wept				
kept				
except				
adopt				
erupt				
fault				
built				
consult				
bolt				
revolt				
difficult				
adult				
left				
loft				
swift				
shift				
craft				
lift				
Rome				
Paris				

Missing Letters

1. Use 'pt', 'lt' or 'ft' to complete the list words.

   (a) consu___ ___

   (b) le___ ___

   (c) adu___ ___

   (d) cra___ ___

   (e) difficu___ ___

   (f) exce___ ___

   (g) ado___ ___

Word Hunt

2. Which list word(s) …

   (a) have two vowels making one sound?

   _____ _____

   (b) rhymes with 'home'? _____

   (c) is the past tense of 'weep'? _____

   (d) is the opposite of 'include'? _____

   (e) is the capital of France? _____

   (f) means what a volcano can do? _____

CROSSWORD

3. Use list words to complete the crossword.

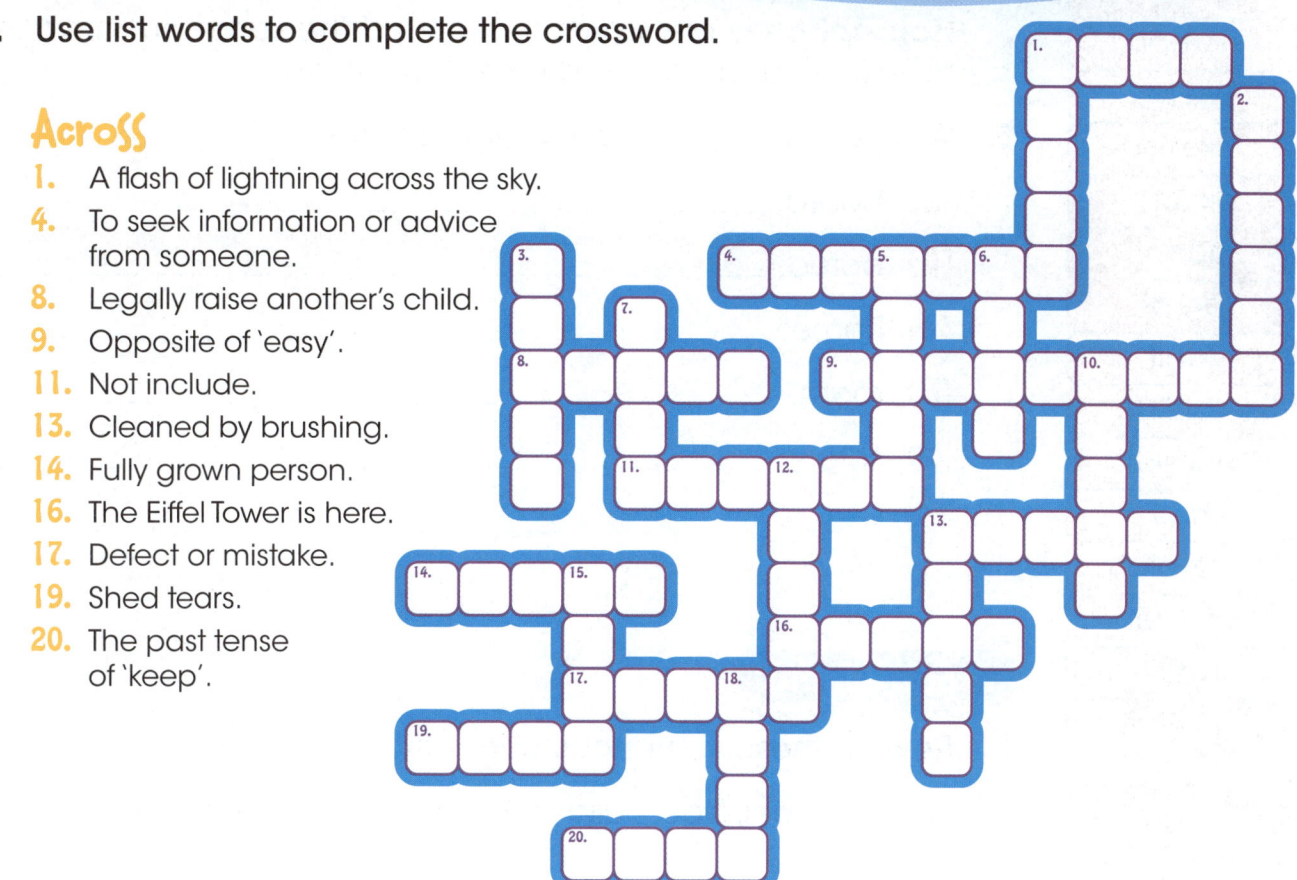

Across

1. A flash of lightning across the sky.
4. To seek information or advice from someone.
8. Legally raise another's child.
9. Opposite of 'easy'.
11. Not include.
13. Cleaned by brushing.
14. Fully grown person.
16. The Eiffel Tower is here.
17. Defect or mistake.
19. Shed tears.
20. The past tense of 'keep'.

Down

1. Constructed.
2. Rebellion.
3. An activity such as pottery, weaving or carving.
5. Move, carry or transfer.
6. Opposite of 'right'.
7. The capital of Italy.
10. Moved slowly and carefully.
12. An active volcano can _____ at any time.
13. Fast, rapid or quick.
15. The space immediately under the roof of a house.
18. Pick up or raise.

Shape Sorter

4. Write the list word that fits in each shape.

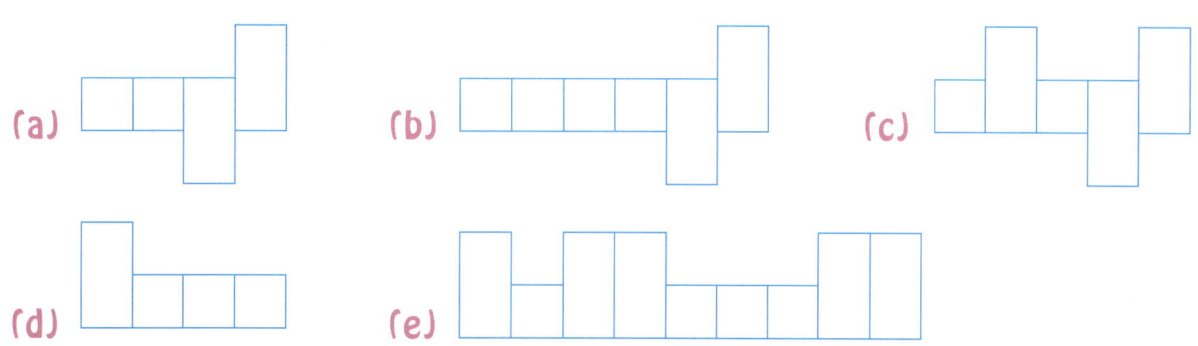

(a)

(b)

(c)

(d)

(e)

Unit 15

pt · lt · ft

List Words

crept
swept
wept
kept
except
adopt
erupt
fault
built
consult
bolt
revolt
difficult
adult
left
loft
swift
shift
craft
lift
Rome
Paris

Revision Words

draw
claw
soar
board
more
score
stalk
chalk
today
year

Homophones

Homophones are words that sound the same but are spelt differently and have a different meaning.

5. Write a sentence for each homophone.

(a) board: _____

(b) bored: _____

(c) Rome: _____

(d) roam: _____

(e) sore: _____

(f) soar: _____

Proofreading

6. Rewrite these sentences correctly.

(a) Last yeer, Dad build us a fantastic den in the lotf.

_____

_____

(b) The cat with the sharp klaw creeped up on the grey mouse.

_____

_____

(c) I would like to drew a sign on that large bored.

_____

_____

Word Meanings

7. Write the list or revision word that matches each meaning.

(a) Ask for specialist advice. _____

(b) Glide high. _____

(c) To try to overthrow a government. _____

(d) To follow somebody secretly. _____

(e) A vessel, ship or boat. _____

WORD SEARCH

8. Find the list and revision words in the word search.

crept	built	swift
swept	consult	shift
wept	bolt	craft
kept	revolt	lift
except	difficult	Rome
adopt	adult	Paris
erupt	left	draw
fault	loft	claw
soar	board	more
score	stalk	chalk
	year	today

```
t l u s n o c k o e r o c s c
o g j m h a r e r u p t g u u
t p e w t e s p h t x r b o g
w b p f v z t t f p m q a t u
c o o o s b a i l j i p v e p
e l l f h t l u c i f f i d y
t t a e i t k e c r e p t i d
l f l w f d l x f i a r o o r
u q i e t d c u j t i f a r a
a f s w r l b h d u y r t o w
f o p a s s i r a a d o p t s
o t o e o h z u d l s i r a P
i b v u m a s o b o k p e x z
o y l o q o t i v e x c e p t
t p e w s p R f r z m o r e a
```

Tenses

To make the past tense of many words, '**ed**' is added; e.g. look — looked.
Sometimes, the word itself is changed; e.g. feel — felt.

9. Complete the tenses below.

Present Tense	Past Tense
(a)	drew
(b) sweep	
(c) creep	
(d) build	
(e) keep	
(f) adopt	

Secret Code

10. Use the secret code to find out the list or revision words.

a	c	d	f	h	k	l	o	r	t	u	y
1	2	3	4	5	6	7	8	9	10	11	12

(a) __ __ __ __ __
   4 1 11 7 10

(b) __ __ __ __ __
   2 5 1 7 6

(c) __ __ __ __ __
   10 8 3 1 12

(d) __ __ __ __ __
   2 9 1 4 10

Additional Activities

11. (a) Write five more capital cities. Check your spelling.

(b) Write the names of the countries they are capitals of.

(c) Choose one of these countries. Research six facts about this country.

Unit 16

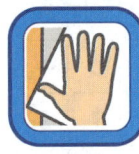

List Words	Practise	Practise	T	D
happily				
merrily				
busily				
angrily				
easily				
cheerily				
craftily				
worried				
married				
dirtied				
copied				
supplied				
dried				
applied				
studies				
carries				
parties				
empties				
buries				
bullies				
litre				
busy				

Missing Letters

1. Fill in the missing vowels to complete the list words.

(a) l__tr___   (b) ___ppl___ ___d   (c) ch___ ___r___ly

(d) b___r___ ___s   (e) d___rt___ ___d   (f) b___sy

(g) ___ngr___ly   (h) b___ll___ ___s   (i) m___rr___ly

(j) w___rr___ ___d   (k) s___ppl ___ ___d   (l) cr___ft___ly

Base Words

2. Write the base words for these.

Most of the list words are made by adding a suffix to a base word ending with the letter 'y'; e.g. happy ⟶ happily.

(a) carries _____   (b) dried _____

(c) copied _____   (d) easily _____

(e) happily _____

CROSSWORD

3. Use list words to complete the crossword.

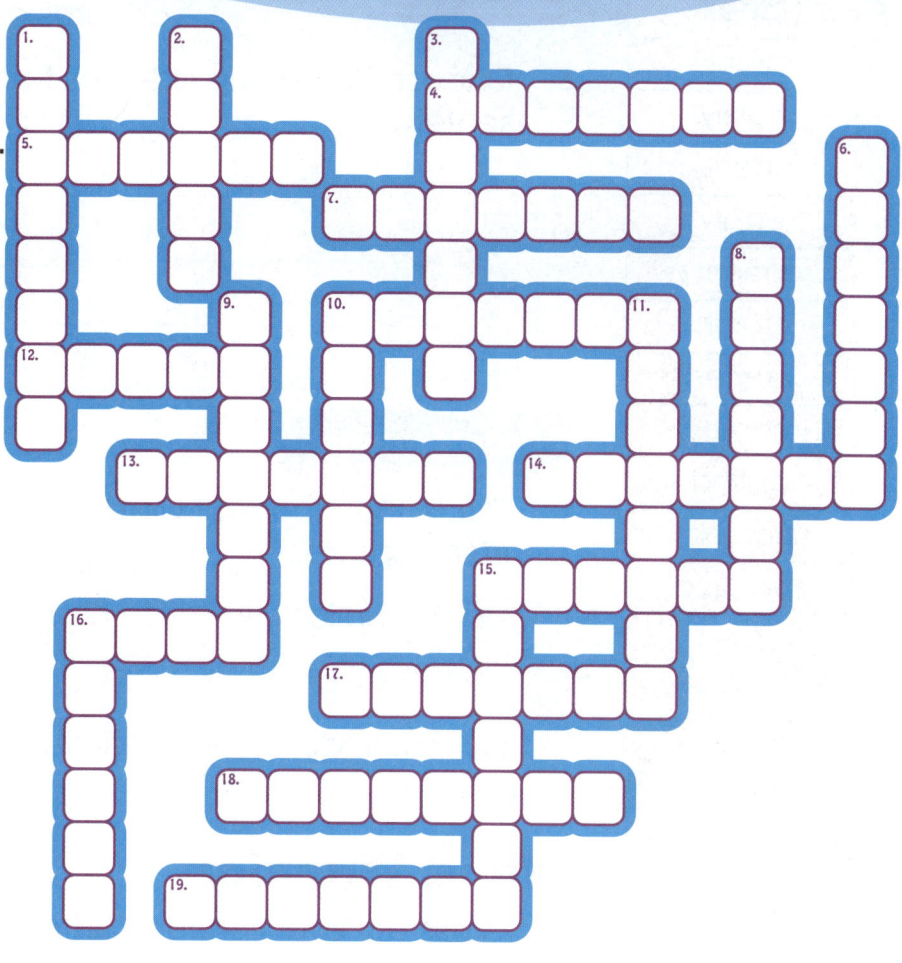

Across

4. The man shouted _____ at the dog.

5. Doing something without great effort.

7. He _____ the brakes quickly to avoid the child.

10. They cause unhappiness or pain.

12. I drink a _____ of water a day.

13. Anxious, distressed or concerned.

14. Opposite of 'fills up'.

15. Made similar to another.

16. Actively doing some kind of work.

17. Joined together as husband and wife.

18. Cunningly.

19. I have been to two birthday _____ this week.

Down

1. Joyfully.

2. Free from moisture or liquid.

3. Cheerfully.

6. My brother _____ every night to pass his exams.

8. Covered or marked with an unclean substance.

9. The girls skipped _____ along the road.

10. My dog _____ his bone in the garden.

11. Provided with something.

15. Moves, takes, shifts or transports.

16. The cooks _____ prepared all the meals.

Tenses

The 'y' at the end of base words changes to 'i' when a suffix is added, except when adding 'ing'.

4. Complete the table.

(a)	worry	worries	worried	worrying
(b)		studies		
(c)		empties		
(d)			married	
(e)			supplied	

Unit 16

List Words

happily
merrily
busily
angrily
easily
cheerily
craftily
worried
married
dirtied
copied
supplied
dried
applied
studies
carries
parties
empties
buries
bullies
litre
busy

Adverbs

An **adverb** is a word that gives information about a verb. Many adverbs end with the letters 'ly'.

5. Choose four of the adverbs from the list and put them in sentences.

- _____
- _____
- _____
- _____

Proofreading

6. Circle the incorrect words and rewrite them correctly in the space.

(a) He aplied himself to his studes and won an ward.

_____ _____ _____

(b) The teacher angrly gave a waning to the billies.

_____ _____ _____

Word Warrior

7. Cross out every second letter to make three list or revision words. _____ _____

_____

rzepwiabrmdnbrutsoypdiryikecdy

Revision Words

reward
warden
award
awkward
warrior
swarm
wardrobe
warning
fortnight
second

Antonyms

8. Write list or revision words with the opposite meanings.

(a) unconcerned

_____

(b) fills

_____

(c) pure

_____

(d) idle

_____

(e) divorced

_____

(f) punishment

_____

(g) sadly

_____

(h) soaked

_____

Suffixes -y words

WORD SEARCH

9. Find the list and revision words in the word search.

happily	married
parties	merrily
dirtied	empties
busily	copied
buries	angrily
supplied	bullies
easily	dried
litre	cheerily
applied	busy
craftily	studies
worried	carries
reward	warden
award	awkward
warrior	swarm
wardrobe	warning
fortnight	second

```
b z y m s y p a r t i e s s x f d
h a p p i l y p b u l l i e s i e
c r a f t i l y k u m a w a r d e
l w l s s v s d v s o f t s a x
k x u a e u x w e c a y i e s p a
u l c g i b m a i u k e c i h p w
a w e n r m d r p y d o l s w l k
w s m e u e e m o v n y v a i i w
o e p d b r i t c d b c r t a e a
r i t r c r l h e l z r r k n d r
r d i a a i p g b r i e r n g y d
i u e w r l p i o o d e i r r a m
e t s i r y u n r e w a r d i j c
d s b q i m s t d b p h x o l r t
z y u z e c f r r d e i r d y l i
l n p w s y m o a c h e e r i l y
w a r n i n g f w f k z o m g g h
```

Word Hunt

10. Which list or revision word(s) …

(a) are units of time?

_____ _____

(b) is a unit of capacity?

_____

(c) has part of your body in it?

_____

(d) has the least number of letters?

_____

(e) starts with 'ch'?

_____

_____

(f) have the word 'or' in them?

_____

_____

_____

Changing Words

11. Change one letter in each word to make a list or revision word.

(a) fried _____

(b) bush _____

(c) studied _____

(d) worries _____

(e) aware _____

(f) garden _____

Additional Activities

12. (a) Write five sentences with two list or revision words in each. Check your spelling.

(b) Underline the adjectives and adverbs.

(c) Circle the nouns and verbs.

Unit 17

ore oor oar our

List Words	Practise	Practise	T	D
explore				
score				
ignore				
adore				
shore				
chore				
anymore				
store				
door				
moor				
floor				
poor				
uproar				
roar				
boar				
boarder				
oar				
fourth				
court				
pour				
Italy				
Switzerland				

Changing Letters

1. Change one letter in the words below to make a list word. Circle the letter you change.

(a) boat _____ (b) your _____ (c) count _____

(d) pool _____ (e) stare _____ (f) road _____

(g) oak _____ (h) choke _____ (i) flood _____

(j) doom _____

Missing Letters

2. Write 'ore', 'oor', 'oar' or 'our' to complete the list words.

(a) anym___ ___ ___   (b) f___ ___ ___th   (c) m___ ___ ___

(d) expl___ ___ ___   (e) upr___ ___ ___   (f) ign___ ___ ___

(g) d___ ___ ___   (h) b___ ___ ___der   (i) ad___ ___ ___

(j) c___ ___ ___t

CROSSWORD

3. Use list words to complete the crossword.

Across

4. To keep things for future use.

5. Next one after third.

8. A European country with many mountains.

13. Used for rowing a boat.

14. A European country shaped like a boot.

15. To let flow.

17. To investigate or look into.

19. Opposite of 'ceiling'.

20. You can play tennis on this.

Down

1. A routine task.

2. To love or cherish.

3. A high area of uncultivated land.

4. Seaside, beach or coast.

6. A wild male pig.

7. Turmoil, disorder or confusion.

8. The number of points or goals.

9. To pay no attention.

10. The sound made by a lion.

11. I am not going to eat _____ sweets.

12. You can open and close it or knock on it.

16. A pupil who lives in school during term time.

18. Opposite of 'rich'.

Missing Words

4. Complete the sentences using the list words.

(a) _____ is famous for pasta and its capital city, Rome.

(b) It was disappointing to come _____ in the race.

(c) Some of the highest mountains in Europe are in _____.

(d) There was _____ in the dining hall when a barking dog ran through.

(e) Please _____ the noise outside and concentrate on your work.

List Words

- explore
- score
- ignore
- adore
- shore
- chore
- anymore
- store
- door
- moor
- floor
- poor
- uproar
- roar
- boar
- boarder
- oar
- fourth
- court
- pour
- Italy
- Switzerland

Revision Words

- know
- knife
- honest
- ghost
- wreck
- write
- crumb
- comb
- tomorrow
- England

Homonyms

5. Circle the correct word and write it on the line.

(a) I (know, no) _____ how to send an email.

(b) I had to say (no, know) _____ to the invitation to the party.

(c) My sister will (right, write) _____ the invitations to her party today.

(d) If you turn (write, right) _____ at the end of the street you will see the park.

(e) The wild (boar, bore) _____ wandered about looking for food.

(f) They had to (boar, bore) _____ a deep hole in the ground to reach the oil.

Proofreading

6. Unjumble the list and revision words.

(a) romootwr _____

(b) mayoren _____

(c) abrored _____

(d) shogt _____

(e) peexorl _____

(f) Sinterlazdw _____

(g) mcbo _____

(h) naglnEd _____

Word Ghost

7. Cross out every second letter to make three list or revision words.

_____   _____   _____

Compound Words

8. Add a list or revision word to these words to make compound words.

(a) ship_____

(b) _____knob

(c) sea_____

(d) _____board

(e) _____yard

(f) _____room

(g) honey_____

(h) bread_____

WORD SEARCH

9. Find the list and revision words in the word search.

explore	door
oar	score
moor	fourth
ignore	floor
court	adore
poor	pour
shore	uproar
Italy	chore
roar	England
anymore	boar
store	boarder
know	knife
honest	ghost
wreck	write
crumb	comb
tomorrow	Switzerland

q	o	l	g	y	t	y	k	b	y	a	u	r	b	s
f	d	t	h	p	e	r	o	n	g	i	w	a	m	c
e	x	p	l	o	r	e	r	o	o	m	r	o	o	o
l	w	a	e	r	o	d	a	h	q	w	i	r	c	r
S	t	t	s	a	n	y	m	o	r	e	t	t	b	e
w	g	a	v	a	c	u	t	b	p	e	e	o	t	e
i	i	h	l	x	o	m	m	x	v	s	r	m	u	o
t	r	g	o	y	u	u	e	r	i	w	a	o	u	v
z	n	e	k	s	r	h	t	o	f	o	h	r	h	j
E	b	z	d	c	t	s	b	o	u	a	r	r	j	s
r	r	e	k	r	e	m	u	l	p	k	s	o	v	r
l	p	r	u	n	a	r	i	f	r	t	r	w	o	i
a	k	o	o	x	i	o	w	c	o	r	o	o	p	s
n	f	h	u	y	m	f	b	r	a	z	d	q	f	d
d	d	c	o	r	y	l	e	b	r	e	b	o	a	r

Tenses

10. Finish the table by writing the correct tense; e.g. grow, grows, growing, grew.

	Verb	Add 's'	Add 'ing'	Past tense
(a)	store			
(b)	wreck			
(c)	explore			
(d)				knew
(e)				wrote

Additional Activities

11. (a) Write four sentences with two list words in each.

(b) Use a dictionary to write a definition for six list words.

(c) Write the names of ten more European countries.

Unit 18

List Words	Practise	Practise	T	D
barbecue				
steak				
sausages				
charcoal				
lighter				
tennis				
racket				
prawns				
salad				
lakes				
park				
caravan				
jeans				
jumper				
shorts				
sandals				
castle				
postcards				
circus				
umbrella				
Moscow				
Berlin				

Small Words

1. Write the list word that contains these words.

   (a) as _____

   (b) car _____

   _____

   (c) or _____

   (d) and _____

   (e) age _____

   (f) raw _____

Letters into Words

2. Write three list words using the letters in the box.

   _____

   _____

   _____

   g, l, h, s, n, e, r, i, b, t, n

CROSSWORD

3. Use list words to complete the crossword.

Across

3. Made from denim.
5. Uses fresh vegetables.
8. Played with a racket.
9. You tow this on a holiday.
11. Cooked on a barbecue.
12. Largest city in Russia.
13. Seafood.
17. Loud noise or uproar.
18. Worn to keep warm.
20. King and queen live in this.
21. Used to keep dry.

Down

1. Sent in the post.
2. _____ can be dangerous places to swim in.
4. Made from minced meat.
6. We need a _____ to start the barbecue.
7. Footwear.
10. Used to provide heat in a barbecue.
13. I am not going for a picnic in the local _____.
14. Worn in summer.
15. Used to cook on in summer.
16. Capital of Germany.
19. Clowns perform here.

Shape Sorter

4. Write the list word that fits in each shape.

(a)

(b)

(c)

(d)

(e)

(f)

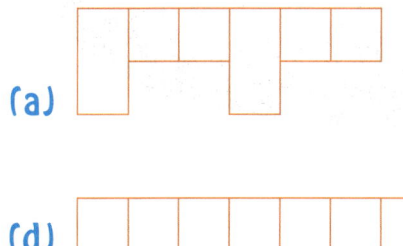
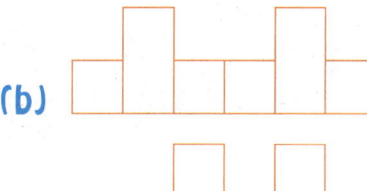
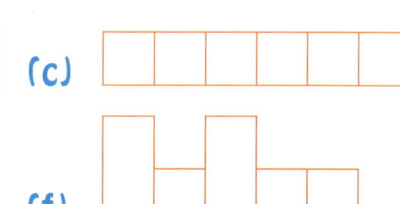

Unit 18

List Words

barbecue
steak
sausages
charcoal
lighter
tennis
racket
prawns
salad
lakes
park
caravan
jeans
jumper
shorts
sandals
castle
postcards
circus
umbrella
Moscow
Berlin

Revision Words

plane
hotel
passport
ticket
beach
boat
uniform
flight
said
there

Picture Story

5. Rewrite the story.
Replace the pictures with a list or revision word.

In America, we saw the , sailed on a

on the _____, and spent the evening at a

on the _____ eating _____.

Rhyming Words

6. Write a list or revision word to rhyme with these.

(a) peach _____   (b) lawns _____

(c) ballad _____   (d) coat _____

(e) head _____   (f) beans _____

(g) kite _____   (h) pain _____

(i) jacket _____   (j) fake _____

Word Sausage

7. Cross out every second letter.
The leftover letters will make three list or revision words.

_____ _____ _____

72

Secret Code

a	e	h	k	l	n	o	p	r	s	t	u	y
1	2	3	4	5	6	7	8	9	10	11	12	13

8. Use the secret code to find out the message.

11 1 4 2   13 7 12 9   8 1 10 10 8 7 9 11

7 6   11 3 2

8 5 1 6 2

WORD SEARCH

9. Find the list and revision words in the word search.

barbecue   steak
sausages   charcoal
lighter   tennis
racket   prawns
salad   lakes
park   caravan
jeans   jumper
shorts   sandals
castle   postcard
circus   umbrella
Moscow   Berlin
plane   hotel
passport   ticket
beach   boat
uniform   flight
said   there

Additional Activities

10. **(a)** Write six more summer holiday words.

(b) Write a postcard to your friend from your holiday. Check your spelling.

(c) Check his or her address in the phone book.

```
          m q u s
          e p w u j
        d f p c a
        t l r a v
        i i a r r n s f
        c g w a j k a v
      t k h n v u b i x
      j e t s a m t d
        t v h n p l
        z d s e e o
        x c t t r e q b
      y c   o s t e a k
          h v a d w m b f
        i g o M o s c o w
          B e r l i n a u
            w b c b s p
            r a c k e t y
            r w y s a i
            h b d l u h c e
      z t u s e w c a n o h
      c h a r c o a l k i r
          i k u z n c i e f t c x
            t t e n n i s g s o s o
          p o s t c a r d s x h c r m
      b a q l u m b r e l l a g t s m
        s a l a d s a u s a g e s e
            k n v p a s s p o r t r
          t e q h e s a n d a l s z j
        x d x s e l t s a c q j p d
      j e a n s   d o p x
    x o e n w   s
```

Difficult Words I Have Found

Word	Practise	Practise	Practise

My Spelling Workbook D—Prim-Ed Publishing—www.prim-ed.com

My Spelling Dictionary Aa to Ff

Aa

Bb

Cc

Dd

Ee

Ff

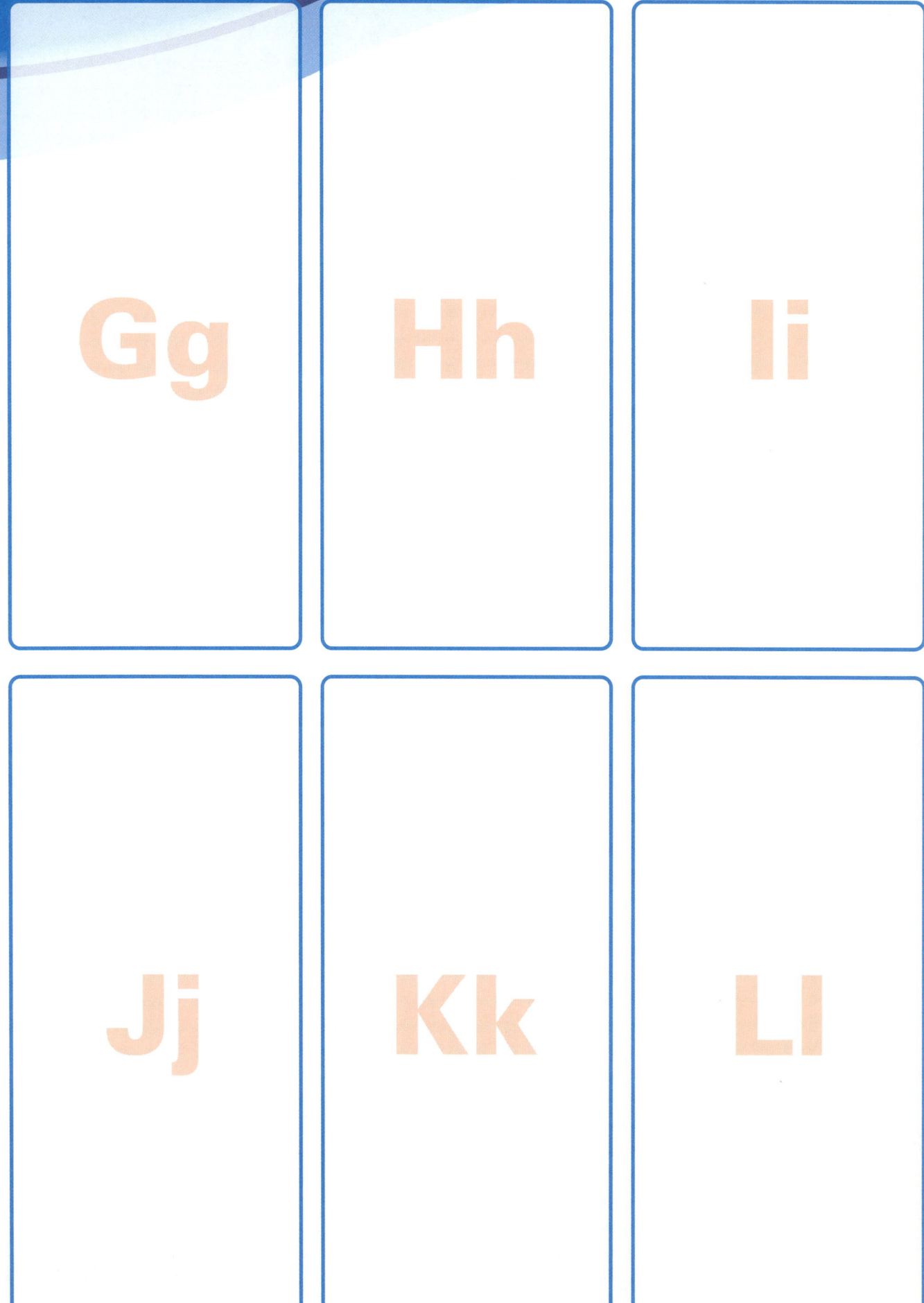

Gg

Hh

Ii

Jj

Kk

Ll

My Spelling Workbook D—Prim-Ed Publishing—www.prim-ed.com

Mm

Nn

Oo

Pp

Qq

Rr

Ss

My Spelling Dictionary Tt to Zz

Tt

Uu

Vv

Ww

Xx

Yy

Zz